SUSAN SLY

INSPIRED TO WIN IN MLM

PROVEN SUCCESS STRATEGIES AND TIPS FROM FAMOUS AUTHORS, TRAINERS AND PEOPLE WHO HAVE ACHIEVED SIX AND SEVEN FIGURE RESULTS

JEFF COMBS • TODD FALCONE • MATTHEW FERRY
JAIREK ROBBINS • MARK VICTOR HANSEN
ERICA COMBS • PK SMITH • DAVID WOOD • T. HARV EKER

Inspired to Win in MLM
Sound Concepts, Inc.
782 S Auto Mall Dr., Suite A
American Fork, Utah 84003

For additional copies of this book please visit www.ReadingIsLeading.com or call
1.888.285.6317

No information contained herein is meant to replace the advice of a doctor or
healthcare practitioner. The data and opinions appearing in this book are for
informational purposes only. Readers are encouraged to seek advice from qualified
health professionals.

ISBN 978-1-933057-85-9

sound*concepts*
creative business solutions

DEDICATION

Who would we ever be without our teachers and the people who believe in us more than we believe in ourselves? Thank you to everyone who has ever given me a kind word or a breath of encouragement. I am grateful to all of the amazing trainers who lent their contribution to this book – Jeff, Erica, Todd, Mark, Harv, Jaerik, David, P.K. and Matthew. Thank you so very much. Most importantly I am grateful to God and my family; I would not be able to do any of the things I do without them.

TABLE OF CONTENTS

Forward by the Author   7

Chapter One
What is MLM?   11

Chapter Two
Your Mindset is What You Take to the Bank   31

Chapter Three
8 Simple Strategies for Reprograming Your Mind   43

Chapter Four
Creating a Plan that Works   73

Chapter Five
The People Business   83

Chapter Six
Creating Your MLM Dynasty   103

Glossary of Terms   112

Recommended Resources   113

About the Author   114

"Anyone who has never made a mistake has never tried anything new."

-Albert Einstein

"I've come to believe that all my past failure and frustration were actually laying the foundation for the understandings that have created the new level of living I now enjoy."

-Tony Robbins

I am perhaps an unlikely candidate to call myself a professional network marketer. In fact, I never would have dreamed that one day I would hear myself say, "I have made millions of dollars in MLM." Growing up, I first dreamed of being a teacher and then a doctor. I was the fat kid, the unpopular kid; the one always picked last for the softball team. In school I was bullied, made fun of and laughed at. It was during this time, feeling as though I didn't fit in, that I found solace in attending the network marketing in-home presentations of my stepmother, Anne.

There, the women always seemed so happy and positive. Even though I was overweight, had buck teeth and long, stringy hair, they told me I was beautiful and smart. I observed these women working hard in their cosmetics company, wanting to better themselves and help others, and I knew that one day I wanted to be just like them. My stepmother eventually ended her network marketing career; however, the impression lasted.

In high school my dad hired me to telemarket and cold call for his company. I humbly say that I became very good at it, methodically dialing the numbers, interviewing the potential clients and setting up appointments. I learned not to be attached to the conversation and that I had to dial a certain amount of numbers before I would find a person willing to give me their information.

"Bubba Sue," my sad school nickname, eventually became just "Sue." I decided to take control of my health, so I took up running and eventually would compete on national teams. I had no idea that my burgeoning athletic mindset would one day assist me in building a million-dollar network marketing business. However, in looking back, the persistence, drive and ability to push past fatigue and pain I learned as an athlete has definitely been useful on many occasions.

I went on to university and completed a science degree. After that I became a personal trainer, guest-lectured at colleges and universities and pursued continued studies in nutrition. I had a passion for bringing people hope with their health problems through nutrition and fitness. I had my daughter, opened a health club, and soon forgot about network marketing until my running coach suggested I enroll in a company with nutritional products that could enhance my performance. However, my coach never truly showed me the business side of the company or taught me about the compensation plan. I liked the products well enough but had no idea what I had access to in network marketing.

In the year 2000 my world turned upside down. I was diagnosed with an illness that would later prevent me from working in the world of fitness. My marriage ended and I lost my business. In a sixteen-week period, I went from being a local media personality, business owner and elite athlete to a single mother without a home or job and over $100,000 in debt. Everything that I had focused on no longer mattered and the reality that I thought existed shattered in a heartbeat.

It's funny sometimes how destiny chooses us, and that is precisely how I came to embrace network marketing as a profession. After losing everything, I found a job working in management for what was then the largest health club chain in the world. It was there, under the pressure of monthly sales quotas, managing a staff of over 50 and working over 70 hours a week, that I met Deborah. I encountered her at a women's networking meeting where I had gone to generate more business for my division. She hired me as her trainer (something I was still doing part-time to make extra money), and over the next eight months she gently prospected me into both a company and an industry.

As I began to truly understand residual income and the possibilities that network marketing held, I embraced the industry. I voraciously read books. I hired coaches. I listened to audios. I went on conference calls. I became ravenous for knowledge. I realized that many of my past experiences, from the in-home presentations with my stepmother to telemarketing to athletics, had prepared me for a career in MLM. I had been developing skills from an early age.

The reality is that we all have skills to contribute to our MLM success—from the parent who is exceptional at organizing his or her children to the police officer who is excellent under pressure. The wonderful thing about this industry is that there are many skills that can be useful in building a solid business. If you have ever had a leadership or teaching position, built systems, run the PTA, organized a golf tournament or even hosted a child's birthday, then you already have strengths that you bring to the table.

In my early network marketing career I decided to "be bad long enough to get good"— a favorite expression of mine. I used every method of recruiting, including lead calling, calling from the phone book, approaching people on the street, talking to family and friends, and running ads. Naturally, I had many frustrating moments and yes, there were times that I wanted to give up and forget about MLM altogether. But I kept on going and that is the ultimate secret to success in anything. I remember doing a presentation on a rainy evening at a chiropractor's office and having one of the participants take me aside and tell me that it was the worst presentation she had ever seen. Times like this were really tough; however, they strengthened my resolve. That woman later joined me in the venture that led me to earn seven figures in MLM, an irony that is still not lost on me today.

There are many different styles of building a network marketing business and if we are truly inspired to win in MLM then we must also understand that different methods serve different people. For some people, a home presentation is their ideal way to build. Others prefer to use social media and the Internet. Regardless of which system you prefer, I encourage you to use many techniques so that you can develop the strengths of the leaders that will come into your team.

My father always taught me that you can lose your job, your company can close, you can come upon hard times; however, no one can take away your skills. If you want to win in MLM, develop your skills. Use the approaches in this book. Learn to understand the industry of network marketing and accept the notion that ultimately we are in the people business. Great network marketers learn to become masterful at developing people and I want to see you become one of the great leaders in our industry.

We have all had our challenging times and you may be in a very hard place right now. Know that every success story happens on the heels of tragedy. One of my favorite sayings comes from Joel Osteen who says, "It is not what we are going through, it is what we are going to." Focus on where, and who, you want to be. Make a decision to be inspired to win in MLM and commit to the journey. The person you become along the way will inspire so many others, and when we are inspiring, people show up to join us.

This book is something I have wanted to write for years. Unlike my other books which focus on women, my desire for this work is to inspire men and women to fall in love with our industry and inspire them to embrace network marketing as a viable profession. The trainers and leaders in this book believe that network marketing can liberate people and families; it is an answer in a bleak economy, a solution to a situation with little hope. Once I was a person with little hope, and this industry saved my life and was an answer to prayer.

Sometimes, the most beautiful gifts arrive in the most unusual packages. My husband once gave me a spectacular watch that he had placed at the bottom of a large box filled with crumpled newspaper. From the outside, the packaging did not seem like much and yet on the inside there was a wonderful gift. Network marketing may very much seem like that box to you. You may have to dig through the newspaper to find the gift but trust me, it is in there.

This industry is more than money and products. It is about people. I have witnessed the most incredible transformations in MLM: women who lacked confidence and had no formal education becoming millionaires; chiropractors and lawyers walking away from jobs that no longer inspired them; families uniting and people discovering their gifts. It is often said that network marketing is a personal development business with a product or service attached and this is very true. You may be in a place right now where the personal growth aspect is what you need more than the contents of a bottle, an educational package, cookware or anything else that is distributed through MLM. What is most exciting is the person you are becoming on the journey right now.

Before our children go to bed every night I say, "You have greatness inside you. You are our gifts from God. You can be, do and have anything you dream." I then ask them, "What are you?" and they reply, "A winner." I ask, "What is your verse?" They say, "He who is within me is greater than he who is in the world." Regardless of whom you call upon – God, your Holy Guardian Angel, Spirit, Source of the Universe – please know that you do have greatness within. You can use MLM to express your greatness and I believe in you. Let's get started on inspiring you to win in MLM.

CHAPTER ONE

WHAT IS MLM?

"Let others lead small lives, but not you. Let others argue over small things, but not you. Let others cry over small hurts, but not you. Let others leave their future in someone else's hands, but not you."

-Jim Rohn

WHAT IS MLM?

MLM, or multi-level marketing, is known by other names. It is sometimes called network marketing or direct selling. This type of selling eliminates the middle man. Goods or services generated by a parent company are brought to the consumer by people like you and me. Instead of paying celebrities and spending multiple millions on advertising (though some MLM companies do), the distributors find the consumers and are remunerated for it.

Direct selling has been around for thousands of years. For ancient peoples, purchasing or bartering goods from a peddler or mobile merchant was very common. In fact, the best advertising was, and still is, word-of-mouth. An ancient Babylonian law even protected these mobile merchants from harm or attack as long as they upheld good morals and ethics. In reality, selling at a fixed retail location is much more recent and especially enhanced by our ability to travel great distances with ease.

Let's talk about the proverbial "elephant in the room." I am of course referring to the notion that MLM is a "pyramid scheme." A pyramid, by definition, occurs when there is a failure of goods or legitimate services to exchange hands. Pyramids or Ponzi schemes also imply that only the person on top can make the most money. A prime example of this would be the notorious financial scandal surrounding investment advisor Bernie Madoff, who was arrested on December 11, 2008 for helming a $65-billion Ponzi scheme that falsely portrayed a legitimate investment house to unfortunate investors. Although some who invested early did receive dividends, those who came in later lost all of their savings. This is an example of a pyramid and should not be compared with legitimate direct-selling companies.

As a side note, I spent a year in corporate America, as a manager at what was then the world's largest health club chain. I often compare the pyramid of a large company to what is absolutely a fairer model with direct selling. For example, in my health club chain there were people who cleaned the facility. They were paid minimum wage. Regardless of how adept they were at cleaning, their chances for advancement to a higher-paying position were very slim. At the next level was front desk staff who greeted the clients. They were paid slightly more than the maintenance workers and were also managed by a person who made only about one dollar more per hour than they did. At the next level were sales people and then a sales manager. There were personal trainers and group exercise instructors. All sales people were managed by someone like me, who made a bonus on their performance, whereas the salespeople themselves could never make a bonus.

In essence, there were many people at the bottom who could never advance unless they went back to school. Managers made bonuses on the performance of others while regional managers received bonuses on these managers. At the top of the pyramid was the CEO of the company and no one could make more money than he did. Unfortunately there is usually only one CEO in any corporate structure. This is truly a pyramid structure and I am grateful that network marketing does not operate in this way.

When you are part of a good company you should have the exact same opportunity to be a top income earner as everyone else. In fact, in an excellent company, your team members should be able to come in and make more money than you are and you would cheer them all the way. In the company where I have made millions of dollars, I actually passed my enrolling sponsor and her sponsor. That, of course, was no accident and in this book, top MLM trainers, leaders and I will share our tips on being inspired to win in MLM. Now that we have had the "pyramid" discussion, let's take a look at the modern history of MLM and why this is considered a legitimate industry.

MLM IN THE LAST 100 YEARS

Multi-level marketing has come under scrutiny due to a lack of understanding and individuals affiliated with companies who promise to make fast and easy money. MLM is not an illegal pyramid scheme if there are actual products exchanging hands. Be wary of companies that remunerate affiliates or associates for recruiting new people only and do not encourage legitimate product users. In 1979, the Federal Trade Commission (FTC) in the United States ruled that Amway was not an "illegal pyramid" per se as there were physical products changing hands and that consumers were in fact able to receive some value even though they were encouraged to find new product users. This forever changed the face of the industry.

There are many legitimate companies out there and the FTC has jurisdiction over multi-level marketing. If a company insists that all affiliates must be re-sellers and have no option to simply purchase products then this can be in violation of the laws governing the industry. If there is not a physical product exchange then this too can be a violation. In fact, many companies have been shut down as they operate as obvious pyramid or Ponzi schemes.

In the last one hundred years, MLM has also seen the rise of extremely solid, product-based companies that yield upward of $100 million in annual sales. From cookware to cosmetics to nutritionals, many network-marketing companies enjoy solid brand-name recognition due to their proven history and track record of integrity. Celebrities, such as Oscar™ award-winning actress Reece Witherspoon, have even been spokespeople for direct-selling companies. Gifted soccer star David Beckham, while playing for the L.A. Galaxy, wears a network-marketing company's logo on his jersey. Network marketing is a legitimate business model and can be extremely liberating when done correctly.

Years ago, franchising was looked upon as a cult. Today, anyone who owns multiple franchises is seen as some sort of entrepreneurial genius despite the fact that it often takes years for a franchise to become profitable. In network marketing, when products are consumable and would be utilized by an individual regardless, there is very little risk involved. Also, profitability can occur much sooner than in franchising when one considers the legitimate tax write-offs that are associated with a home-based business.

Much like it took years for franchising to catch on, the same is true of network marketing. In some countries, it is very common to use MLM as a means of creating another stream of income. In Canada, the United States, Australia and other countries, it is becoming more and more popular. If you are already in a network marketing company or looking for one, be rest assured that when a company contains the key aspects necessary to succeed, the benefits are far greater than simply financial gain.

WHAT CHARACTERISTICS DEFINE A GOOD MLM COMPANY?

There is much opinion, some valid and some not, on the characteristics that would define a good network marketing opportunity. For the purpose of this section, I would like to focus on some defining characteristics that are necessary for an MLM to operate legally, as well as some additional factors that I have observed to be helpful in selecting the right opportunity. Choosing a good company is the first key step in the journey. When you find the right company and you become the right person…that is when the magic happens. Let's take a look at the defining characteristics of a good company and consider some great questions to ask when choosing the right one.

- There must be a physical product or service. Nutritionals, cosmetics and household goods are the most popular. Some long standing companies also provide services such as health insurance, education savings plans and legal advice. Please do your research on a service-based company. Find out how long the company has been in business, who some of their clients are and if they have ever received a letter from the FTC.

- The company must not be making unsubstantiated claims such as, "This juice cures cancer." The FDA will first fine the company and then the company can be shut down.

- There must be a buyer program. People must be able to purchase goods and services without having to distribute.

- A company must provide excellent training and ideally have the most fundamental training available without additional cost.

- The company must have the infrastructure in place to meet demand.

- A company that has industry experts and/or people with a successful background in direct selling has advantages because corporate decisions affect the field.

- Many companies go out of business within their first two years, so choosing a company that is two years or older can have certain advantages.

- In this era, a company with a strong Internet presence is essential.

- A company that has consumables ensures that some consumers will re-order.

- The compensation plan must be fair. Is there an opportunity for a new distributor to out-earn their sponsor?

- Does the compensation plan require distributors to give away sponsorships to their upline team members? This has many disadvantages.

- Can an affiliate make money simply by retailing or do they have to physically enroll new members before their commissions begin? Be leery of any company that does not allow for retail direct sales to consumers.

- Look at the Income Earnings Disclosure statement for the company.

- If the company is publicly traded, do your research on their stock performance.

- Does the company have evidence that people are making the type of income that is being promoted?

- If possible, check out a local presentation and meet some of the people who are already involved.

- Does the company require distributors to continually personally enroll new members in order to get paid? If so, there isn't true residual income.

- Does the company encourage personal growth?

- Are the leaders/owners of the company ethical? Do not hesitate to Google or use other Internet search engines to research the people at the top.

- Can you see yourself staying with this company for years?

- Is the product/service something you would use yourself?

- Is the company registered with the Better Business Bureau?

- Does the company encourage a form of marketing that you can utilize?

For example, some companies encourage home presentations exclusively. If this is not something you can embrace then it may not be a good fit. The same is true if the company suggests only online marketing and you are not savvy in that area. A good company has something that can be marketed using a variety of methods to be more inclusive.

Lastly, do your homework. If possible, interview distributors who are with the company you are considering. When researching a company online, understand that everyone has an opinion and people who have negative opinions may not necessarily be presenting biased or anecdotal evidence. If you are dealing with a product-based company, always try the product before you consider the business. If you do not believe in the products you will have a difficult time endorsing them.

When you find the right company, focus in. There will always be promises of easy money and some may appear enticing. Anyone who achieves a significant, sustained income in network marketing focuses on one company. While some people may have one or two good months or even a good year, the key to long-term residual income is staying the course in one opportunity.

INSPIRED TO WIN IN MLM TIP

Know the characteristics of a good company. When you find one...stay with it.

HOW DO NETWORK-MARKETING COMPANIES PAY OUT THEIR COMPENSATION PLANS?

We can all agree that we are in an age where computers can take data and produce quantifications at frightening speeds. In order to understand how a company pays out their distributors you may want to think like a computer.

Every time a person purchases an MLM product or service there is an associated volume or dollar amount. Computers can also calculate the percentage of people that are likely to recruit others and the percentage of people who are going to simply use the products or services. Because of this level of certainty computers basically can figure out how many people will get paid on a given transaction.

Compensation plans all have defaults which ensure stability. Some of the older compensation plans have a "breakaway" which essentially stops paying the upline on an associate whose volume begins to exceed theirs. Other compensation plans pay only to a certain level of depth. Others still require a minimum number of legs to hit a certain level of volume in order for the upline to receive the maximum pay-out. Almost every compensation plan has a minimum monthly requirement to ensure compensation and, though this varies from company to company, it generally ranges from $150 to $300 per month.

Any company that has been in business for a minimum of two years without missing a paycheck has created safeguards to ensure stability. It is very common in MLM for a new company to create an outrageous compensation plan in order to lure people in. As more people join and force the commissions, the company will usually change the compensation plan and this can occur even in the pre-launch stage. I have actually heard of companies who change the compensation plan two or three times before products actually begin shipping.

Lastly, every successful MLM is run like a big business. It may either have a board of directors to which it is accountable, or be publically traded. Both situations can create a small measure of assurance that a compensation plan is able to do what it says it can. Like all large companies, MLMs generally re-invest a portion of profits into research and development, as well as have expenses such as payroll, technical support, licensing, insurance, rent and the other day-to-day costs of doing business. A company will have these same expenses whether it sells its vitamins at Wal-Mart or from a network-marketing company. The fundamental difference is that most network-marketing companies use their marketing, sales and retail location budget to pay people just like you and me. We can continue to shop at large stores; however, we are very unlikely to get our products paid for or generate a significant, life-changing income. By supporting network marketing we support other individuals just like us.

CAN ANYONE SUCCEED IN NETWORK MARKETING?

Every year, all over the world, people enroll in network-marketing programs. Some join for the products, some for the business. Others still join for both. Perhaps you are already in a network-marketing company or maybe you are considering one. Regardless of what compelled you to pick up this book, know that individuals just like you do in fact make it in MLM.

You may be wondering if you can actually create a solid income in network marketing and the answer is absolutely, "Yes." People just like you are drawn to this extremely accepting industry. If you went to any of the top network-marketing companies' conferences you would find a beautiful diversity of people. There are people in their twenties, right up to their eighties and nineties. There are people in wheelchairs, those who are visually or hearing-impaired. There are people from various countries of origin in a wonderful array of skin tones. There are same-sex couples, single mothers, single fathers, traditional couples, and families of all kinds.

The diversity is also apparent when it comes to education. I have known several network-marketing millionaires who had only a high school diploma. I have also met seven-figure-income earners with more than one university degree. I have spoken at network-marketing events attended by physicians, lawyers, accountants, engineers, teachers, chiropractors and other professionals simply looking to create an exit strategy. I have met and mentored several who have succeeded and created six and seven-figure incomes.

On a daily basis, I encounter people who attempt to create an excuse as to why they cannot succeed in this industry. The truth is that our excuses are nothing more than false realities we choose to live in as a lame attempt to keep us stuck. We will cover this in more depth in the chapter on mindset. When we want something badly enough there can be no excuses. If we have a burning desire in our heart to succeed then no matter our circumstance—whether we be black, white, Asian, Hispanic, educated, non-educated, have children, or not—we must commit to pressing forward if we truly want to create a better life for ourselves.

One of my dear friends and mentors, Jimmy Smith, is 82 years old at the writing of this book. He is the top income earner in his company, making millions of dollars every year. Jimmy joined that company at age 74, leaving behind a six-figure income in another company. Even though people told him that he was crazy to leave that company at his age, he followed his heart and his dream to make a seven-figure annual income in MLM.

You see, Jimmy operates in the realm of "no excuses." He does not think of himself as limited by his age. Every challenge, he feels, is an opportunity to stretch and grow. Jimmy feels that being in his eighties is a gift because it gives him a greater sense of urgency. Jimmy is fearless.

You may have been passed over for a job, promotion or an opportunity because of your lack of education or other circumstances. This will not happen in network marketing. You see, in MLM, we become our own boss. We decide how much we are worth. We choose our path to greatness.

Can you succeed here? The evidence is real that the answer is "Yes." People just like you are inspired to win in MLM every single day. You can absolutely be successful here. There is a wonderful industry awaiting you and this book will provide the tools to help you select a great company and build a solid team. Let's get started.

Inspired to Win in MLM Tip
Anyone can succeed in the industry if they stick with it long enough and operate from a consistent realm of "no excuses."

DIRECT SELLING BY THE NUMBERS

People often have stereotypes of who participates in network marketing. We think of images of women taking cosmetics door-to-door or the slick salesperson doing a whiteboard presentation to a group of surprised friends and relatives. Today's MLM is the antithesis of these images and in reality you might be surprised at the demographics of the industry. As of 2009, 74 percent of Americans had used direct-selling products of some sort. Of that percentage, 80 percent reported a positive experience.

According to the Direct Selling Association in America, over 16 million people participated in direct selling in 2009 and that was up 6.6 percent over the previous year. According to the World Federation of Direct Selling Associations, as of 2008 there were 65 million people in the world participating in multi-level marketing and direct sales. That number continues to climb. In 2009, direct sales outperformed retail sales. Although both experienced declines in overall sales due to a much weakened economy, the direct-selling industry saw only a 4.3 percent drop, while retail sales fell by 7.3 percent. Although people were losing jobs at a record pace, there was an increase of 1 million people entering the direct-selling profession.

In 2009, approximately 65 percent of the industry was made up of products affiliated with wellness, personal care and home goods. 78.1 percent of all sales were done face-to-face. That is a major indicator that to truly be inspired to win in MLM one must master person-to-person connecting.

In America, over 80 percent of the direct-selling force is women. The prime demographic tends to be those in the age range from 35 to 54, although there is a considerable representation from those ages 18 to 34. 92 percent of direct sellers build a business part-time and almost 80 percent of consumers report that they are primarily product users.

Globally, as of 2009, direct selling was a burgeoning $115-billion-per-year industry. To give you some perspective, in 2009, Nike Shoes' global revenue was $19.2 billion. Nike of course is a brand name with global recognition and a mega giant in the footwear and athletic apparel industry. Everyone knows the Nike swoosh and yet very few people truly understand and appreciate network marketing and direct sales.

Inspired to Win in MLM Tip
Know the numbers of the direct selling and multi-level marketing industry.

Statistics from the Direct Selling Association fact sheet for 2009.

WHAT DO THESE STATISTICS REALLY TELL YOU?

The number of people participating in network marketing is growing. Most people are attracted to companies that offer a specific product that is consumable, in personal care or for the home. This is why so many women participate in the industry as women are very accustomed to word-of-mouth and referral marketing. From a business standpoint it is important to understand that 80 percent of your organization will be happy to simply use the products. If you can provide an emotional tie to your product then the likelihood of creating a long-term, sustainable business is greatly increased.

I have also co-written a book called *MLM Woman*. I would recommend this if you are serious about the industry as chances are the majority of your organization will indeed be women.

THE GLOBAL ECONOMY AND WHY MLM

Truthfully, in the coming years as the Baby Boomers (those born between 1946 and 1964) look to retire, the economy will transition greatly. Great financial authors such as Robert Kiyosaki of *Rich Dad Poor Dad* -fame predict that Americans will be severely challenged as this age group begins to pull its assets out of the stock market. In 2008 and 2009, the world experienced a massive recession. The Baby Boomers themselves saw their savings decline and made some key decisions which affected all of the other generations.

Many Baby Boomers decided to stay in their jobs longer, leaving fewer openings for the next generation, known as "Generation X." Generation X refers to those born from 1961 to 1981 and is known as the "Baby Bust" because of the decline in births over that time period. Although they may be small in numbers, many in this group, while still paying off student loans, were forced to stay in lower paying positions already holding a mortgage and likely with a young family. Many were laid off and economists warned that more would come. In 2010, the economy did begin to recover, however the markets ebbed and flowed much like the most terrifying roller coaster you can imagine.

As people lost their homes, went further into debt, and governments overextended themselves with bailouts, one industry silently provided options to people all over the world facing financial uncertainty. That industry, of course, is network marketing, which attracted people of all ages looking for an alternative. Even those who were previously opposed to joining a network-marketing company looked to it for a "Plan B."

The reality is that times have changed. For my parents' generation the solution was to go to school, get good grades and get a job that had a pension. That is no longer the reality as many pension funds are overstressed, people are being taxed at record levels and the average person can barely keep up. Many jobs do not offer pensions and those that do require decades of employment which comes at a cost. The opportunity costs are less time with families, little time to take care of our health, and increased stress. Network marketing, when done right, is a viable solution to the financial challenges people are facing all over the world.

With "Generation Y" coming of age, we are seeing greater numbers of people born after 1981 joining network-marketing companies. Many students are graduating university with slim prospects for a career. As Generation X loses jobs and clings to their current positions awaiting the Baby Boomers to retire, they also take on lower position jobs in an effort to stay afloat. This leaves Generation Y with fewer prospects. With the age of social media and the non-negotiable Internet, Generation Y is primed to build in direct sales especially with companies that are Internet-savvy.

As we look back at this time in history, I believe we will see how the economy shifted the landscape of network marketing. In this book you will find stories of people who have achieved six-figures-plus incomes in MLM and transcended their economic status. You will learn tips on how to build an inspired business and also learn from the top network-marketing trainers. Along the way, I will weave in my own story and how I have come to make millions of dollars in the industry, retire my husband (a chartered accountant) and raise our children with a prosperity mindset.

Inspired to Win in MLM Tip
With economic uncertainty and legitimate companies emerging as safe havens, the reality is that MLM is going to continue to grow.

EVERYTHING HAPPENS FOR A REASON

If you are like me, then you also believe that everything happens for a reason. I believe that you are reading this book for a reason. I hope that you are already inspired to win in MLM. Perhaps you are a little uncertain. Maybe you feel you require more skills. You could be looking for a company or you could already be successful and wanting to get to the next level. Wherever you are know that I, along with the other trainers and authors in this book, believe that you can win in MLM. You are part of a changing economic landscape and direct selling is a major force providing solid options for people who previously lacked hope.

Throughout this book there are success stories from people just like you who have been inspired to win in MLM. They come from different companies, backgrounds, age groups and professions. The only common denominator is that they see MLM as a viable profession that has absolutely transformed their lives. Additionally you will be offered tips from the top MLM trainers including Jeffrey Combs, Todd Falcone, Matthew Ferry, Jairek Robbins and *Chicken Soup for the Soul* co-author Mark Victor Hansen.

Lastly, as someone who has been inspired to win in MLM, please know that I believe you can make it in this industry. Network marketing is one of the only mediums where ordinary people just like you and me can make extraordinary incomes. Let's get started on your journey to success and set you up to win in MLM.

FIELD SUCCESS
JASON L. – GENERATION Y SUCCESS

When I was 18 years old, I had blue hair, spent my Friday and Saturday nights in the library, and was deathly afraid to making eye contact with people of authority. In fact, when four suitemates piled into the backseat of a white '94 Honda Civic and asked me to come along to an "opp. meeting," I was too shy to say "No."

That initial meeting forever changed my life. I didn't sleep for three days. Up until that point, it never occurred to me that I could take control of my time and money. It was second nature: wake up, go to school, wake up, go to work. That is just what everyone did. But in the world of network marketing, a few hundred dollars and some sweat equity could create an asset that would pay me months after for work I did today. I could build a company of thousands without the initial capital of a traditional business. And best yet, if I grew leaders, I could eventually achieve time and money freedom.

So began my love of network marketing. During the day I was reading microeconomics, but by night I was devouring pages by Robert Kiyosaki, Napoleon Hill, and Dale Carnegie. Unfortunately my first four years in network marketing were just that, reading. It came as no surprise that my largest monthly check at the time was $350.

As fate would have it, our network marketing company was bought and acquired. Seven friends and I found ourselves in a unique position: hit our target goals or the company would be gone. In 11 months, I went from a struggling 23-year-old, to making a six-figure annual income. I would later go on to become the top income earner, become the company's top trainer, and help multiple people achieve six-figure annual incomes.

Looking back now at almost a decade in the industry, I've been fortunate enough to experience some of the wonder that caught my eye when I was 18 years old. My wife and I were fortunate enough to take a month-long honeymoon in the countryside of Sienna, Italy. And yes, we came back to a larger check than the month prior. But what keeps me coming back for more is the possibility of choice and creating choices for others. In places where most of us feel as though there are never enough hours in the day, I cannot tell you how gratifying it is to not commute to work. In network marketing you can choose how much your time is worth. And as my wife and I begin to plan for parenthood, it is network marketing that has given us the choice to be full-time parents.

Whether you are beginning this journey at 18 or 88, stick with it. Find the best mentors possible, learn daily, and keep taking action. I wish all of you an amazing journey as you create your life by design.

FIELD SUCCESS
CHRIS - LIFE LESSONS THAT HAVE HELPED ME IN NETWORK MARKETING

Having gone pretty much broke with my real estate investments, I turned to network marketing. The headaches of dealing with employees, subcontractors and all the overhead associated with real estate and conventional business drove me to seek other options. I learned that I no longer wanted or needed that stress.

Network marketing has allowed my wife and I to work together (instead of apart with the stress of conventional business), travel together and to build an income that went from zero dollars to between sixty and eighty thousand dollars monthly in just 22 months. Where else can you do that without investing hundreds of thousands if not millions of dollars?

I'm now super happy that the real estate market took a turn. Instead of dealing with a competitive environment, network marketing is the healthiest environment offered in any business as it only grows by helping each other and developing teams. Having now been with my company for 24 months, my big "A ha!" moment came through realizing the simplicity of the following questions that everyone should be asking themselves:

1. *If I keep doing exactly what I'm doing with my current income generating vehicle, will I be thrilled with my results? In real estate our answer was "No."*

2. *If I stop working or building my business, will my income sustain itself or, even better, grow? Our answer was "No" — it was completely contingent upon our work.*

3. *Do I have the chance to work with the very best in my business and not have to pay for that coaching? Our answer was "No."*

TRAINING TIP
BY MASTER TRAINER JEFFERY COMBS
SEVEN KEYS TO SUCCESS

We all have a desire to achieve success. For some the desire is greater than the average person. Let's face it, everyone wants to be successful but very few are really willing to do W.E.I.T. (What Ever It Takes). I have assisted thousands of entrepreneurs through my seminars, workshops, and personal coaching programs and I have found that there are a few key principles that assist people in achieving the levels of success that they deserve.

1. Success is an Attitude
This attitude is a posture that you take that states, "I deserve to have it all." Success is a habit and has no real secrets. It all starts with your belief system. Your belief system starts with how you feel about yourself. Your personal self-esteem is the key ingredient to attaining the success you seek.

2. Living in the Past is a Recipe for Failure
Forgiving yourself, others in your past, past mistakes, and failures

is paramount in your early journey to success. You attract to your reality who and what you are. When you are positive and feel good about you, you attract like-minded individuals. The same holds true if you are negative in your thought processes. Your thought processes will always determine your bank account of love. It is essential that you learn to forgive, let go, and let go of your past.

3. Success is a Process, Not a Payoff

Success is a process, not a payoff. You will pay your ten dollars at the door on your journey to success, and you will find out quickly that there are no shortcuts. You will never be able to completely master every detail of your life. Attempting to do so will only lead to frustration. What will make the most difference is becoming the master of a few key principles that will allow you to have the fastest personal growth.

4. Think Big – Act Big

When you begin to think exponentially instead of incrementally, you have begun. Life and people will never give you what you don't ask for. However, life will give you exactly what you demand of it. As you repair your self-worth, you will feel good about asking for what you know you deserve. As you think big, you see that you deserve more. Thinking big allows you to accomplish in days what would have taken years.

5. Always read the MAP!

In other words, have a plan of action. If you can't tell someone exactly how you will reach a goal, then you never will! The first step in creating your map to success is to decide on the destination— the goal. Your goals should be clear, precise, and realistic, yet high enough so you stretch to reach them.

6. Act Consistently

By taking the daily plan of action and extending it so that you have a seven-day schedule, you know exactly what you will do for the entire week This frees up your energy so that each day you can put the administrative tasks aside and simply begin achieving!

7. Break Goals Down to "The Ridiculous"

No matter what business you are in, the most important aspect will be collecting the results. Breaking your goals down to "the ridiculous" means taking a big goal and understanding what incremental actions are required on a daily, weekly, or monthly basis to create the results required to achieve your ultimate objective.

For more information, please visit www.GoldenMastermind.com where Jeff's resources will teach you to master the core principles you require to release procrastination and achieve any goal ... and assist you to develop your personal action plan to increase your results and income, create more free time, and allow you to enjoy more fun and less stress!

Jeffery Combs is an internationally recognized speaker, trainer, and author, specializing in prospecting, leadership, personal break-throughs, prosperity consciousness, spiritual enlightenment, mind-set training, and effective marketing. His training revolves around personal growth and development, cuts to the chase, and delivers information that makes an immediate impact on your success! Jeff can be contacted online at www.GoldenMastermind.com, or toll free at 800-595-6632.

TRAINING TIP
WITH MASTER TRAINER AND AUTHOR ERICA COMBS

AN EMPOWERING NETWORK MARKETING MINDSET FOR WOMEN

Regardless of your personal history, deciding to embark in your journey as a business owner can feel very intimidating. This being said, the world of entrepreneurship is full of exciting and boundless possibilities, especially the opportunity to become a leader and assist other women to step into leadership positions. After all, ladies, we constitute 82 percent of the network marketing industry — it's time to move into the top-ten percentage of income earners. We've been commanding the retail markets for years; it's time to get paid like a Corporate Executive!

This transition will require a willingness to not just lead and command the market, but to assist others to realize and actualize their leadership potential as well. Leadership is often misconstrued as a daunting task full of responsibilities and obligations. The truth is that true leadership begins with a willingness to investigate your strengths and then learn how to teach those strengths to the people who desire the results you have achieved and are willing to follow your system and discover their strengths along the way. Whew! That takes the pressure off you!

Here are a few simple tips to consider and perhaps journal your feelings about to embark on your journey as a leader:

1. Start Looking for an Opportunity to Lead
Where can you be of service in your business? It may sound like a contradiction, however all leadership grows from a seed of service to a greater community. It is in this service that we create our special niche of value and discover our natural strengths, abilities, and realize what we enjoy doing!

2. Open Your Mind to Exploring a New Adventure
In the beginning, consider the idea of leadership— what it means to you, what value it will bring to your life, and the value you will bring to others. This is a great place to journal, and it is always liberating to explore your feelings.

3. Identify and Acknowledge Your Strengths
One way to significantly increase your confidence when you enter any new endeavor is to acknowledge the strengths you currently have. These are the skills you have already developed through your life experiences, perhaps as a business woman, teacher, parent, etc. Take a moment to list ten skills or strengths you currently possess. It is so empowering to recognize and acknowledge the skills you do have, and then consider how these skills can benefit you as you continue to develop other skills you know you require.

4. Grab a Girlfriend and Ask Her to Hold You Capable

Yes, that's right! Create a forum of support as you progress – this is someone to share victories and frustrations with, someone with whom you can be honest without fear of judgment. Ask her if you can connect with her each week to share your journey and lend you the encouragement you seek to move forward – I guarantee she will inspire you, feeding your spirit to inspire others.

Erica Combs, Vice President of Golden Mastermind Seminars, Inc. is the author of the best-selling book, *Women In Power: A Woman's Guide to Free Enterprise.* She can be contacted online at www.GoldenMastermind.com or toll free at 800-595-6632.

CHAPTER TWO

YOUR MINDSET IS WHAT YOU TAKE TO THE BANK

"We see what we believe."

-Wayne Dyer

TAKING 100% RESPONSIBILITY FOR YOUR LIFE

The road to winning in MLM doesn't actually begin with the people you enroll, it begins with your mindset and that means that you have to take 100-percent responsibility for every thought, action and belief that you have. To truly succeed in this industry your mind will have to be stronger than the obstacles that you encounter. Believe me, there will be challenges. People often quit when their friends turn down the opportunity to get started in their enterprise or when their families are not supportive of MLM. In fact, many people will use this as an excuse as to why they cannot succeed when the reality is that it has nothing to do with anyone other than the person in the mirror.

I was once on a training call for master MLM coach Jeffrey Combs. We were discussing how people often struggle in this industry because of their issues with anger, the root of which is disappointment. I shared that for years I had been the type of person who was able to produce results out of anger; I was always looking to prove myself. That mindset got me to six figures; however, I did not progress further until I learned to step into a greater place of peace and compassion. I had always thought that production from peace was for the weak until I met Jim Rohn, one of the most peaceful people I had ever encountered. Mr. Rohn, who passed in 2009, was an incredible speaker, author and business philosopher. He had such an aura of peaceful power about him that I decided, then and there, to simply surrender to the journey of letting go of my anger.

Abandoned and sexually abused as a child, I had struggled to prove myself for my entire life. When I competed in a race, I always wanted to be faster. When I had a report card with straight As, I wanted straight A-pluses. You see, it was never enough and I brought that mindset into network marketing. I would enroll people, go to the ends of the Earth for them and then set myself up to be disappointed when they left my organization. Instead of looking internally for ways to improve, I looked externally when things were going wrong. Instead of taking 100-percent responsibility for my life, I blamed my upline for where I had been placed, I blamed my financial situation on having MS, I blamed my weight on poor genetics…you get the picture.

I was a victim and not a victor. Jeff, who was first my coach and now one of my best friends, told me that vulnerability and weakness were not the same thing. He said that if I wanted to win in the industry, and he believed I would make over a million per year, that I would have to let down my barriers and come from a place of vulnerability. In other words, the perfect image I thought I was portraying as a person who had all of the answers was really a facade. He said that although I could attract some followers and was already making six figures, I would never truly get to the next level until I began to open up and let people see some of the pain I had been through.

I admit that the journey from that place— a place where I had locked up all of my pain in a dark little corner of my soul— to where I am today was one of the most challenging things I have ever done. I once came in eighth place in the pro division of the Ironman triathlon in Malaysia with a fractured pelvis and releasing my anger eclipsed that physical pain one-thousand fold.

We all have challenges. We all have our stories of why we cannot succeed. Some of us believe that our parents were "fishing in the shallow end of the genetic gene pool" and this is why we are overweight and unhealthy as opposed to owning our "stuff," so to speak. Many people feel that they are victims of debt and blame the economy for their financial mishaps. Other people still blame people in their relationships for hurt, anger and frustration when the reality is that every relationship takes two.

This may be tough to absorb, but if you truly want to win in MLM you are going to have to take 100-percent responsibility and own every aspect— good and what you perceive as bad— about your life. From your weight to your bank account to your relationship status, no one else is to blame for any of it. It is entirely up to you. You may want to put this book down. Years ago, I would have, however master-trainer Tony Robbins says, "When we think we can't that is when we absolutely must."

I believe that you are destined to win in MLM and that although your journey may be challenging I encourage you to keep going. Starting right now, give up blame, judgment and jealousy. Own every aspect of your life and consider it a starting place. You are absolutely the author of your own success story and you are about to write a new chapter.

Inspired to Win in MLM Tip
Take 100% responsibility for your life. Give up judgment, blame and jealousy. These are all seductive traps that keep us angry and stuck.

YOUR UNTRAINED PUPPY

Your mind is not your best friend. In fact it can be your worst enemy unless it is well trained. An untrained mind will often tell you to give up, stop dreaming and seduce you into losing focus. Your mind is like a brand new, untrained puppy. It may appear cute but the reality is that it will pee on the new rug, chew your designer shoes and inevitably keep you up at night. Your untrained puppy of a mind is quick to lose focus and fast to zero in on the newest, shiniest thing available. Until you train your puppy, you will lose your inspiration to win in MLM.

I have encountered many talented people who jumped from opportunity to opportunity much like the puppy jumping on its master. Even though these incredible people could prospect and close, their untrained minds led them down the path of destruction causing them to experience self-sabotage. Your mind will tell you to give up, get out of MLM and suggest you sit on the sofa and watch re-runs of your favorite television show or surf the Net looking at the news.

Every successful person has had experience with their own untrained puppy of a mind. Anyone who has ever successfully maintained a six or seven-figure income in MLM has had to face their "puppy" head on and take control. Only through discipline developed by consistently reading books, listening to audios, attending live events and the willingness to do the work, will you ever become the master of your mind; until then your mind will be master over you.

Your mind is not your best friend. It is like an untrained puppy creating mayhem in your life. If you want to win in MLM then you have got to train the puppy.

TAKING CONTROL OF YOUR MIND

Years ago I ran a Robb Report ad that said, "Heart of a champion, want the bank account of one?" It was a simple little ad that pulled about ten or more qualified leads per month. I chose the Robb Report because the readership already had a mind that was tuned to prosperity. If you have never read a Robb Report, I highly recommend it. Monthly features include things like "the best private jets" or "the best yachts." You can understand why I would market there: the people were already associating themselves with the best of the best and my little business-opportunity ad fit in nicely.

The vast majority of people are not dialed-in to the mindset of a champion. They live their lives as though it is a matter of surviving and not one of thriving. People allow themselves to become victims of the economy, their past, relationships and their health. The reality is that the average American is overweight and broke. In the documentary *Super Size Me,* it stated that the average American consumed fast food at least two times per week. The USDA says that the average American receives over one-third of their calories away from home. What does this all mean? It means that Americans are stressed for time if they are eating out so much, they are gaining weight at a rapid pace and the average debt per person is climbing.

If you are serious about winning in MLM it means that you will have to "go against the grain," so to speak. With only about five percent of Americans earning over $100,000 per year, your MLM venture with a mindset on prosperity is already challenging to the majority of people out there. When you turn on the news, you see and hear negativity. When you read the newspaper, you also read about wars, crime and debt. Bad news sells and good news does not.

Most people are programmed to believe that they are not exceptional. They are taught to believe the status quo. If you grew up in a family where you were taught to go to school, get good grades and find a job with a pension, then you were in the majority. The reality is that this type of thinking does not usually create some sort of entertainment of the notion that one can get ahead by investing in a network-marketing business. This is what most of our minds are programmed for – survival. If you want to win in MLM you have got to reprogram your mind to thrive.

One of the first things I suggest to people is to stop reading newspapers or watching the news for the first 90 days of their MLM venture. You may be saying, "Susan – you are crazy. I can't live in a bubble." My answer to that is, "Says who?" Until you train your mind to be disciplined, positive and coachable, you cannot afford to be exposed to any negativity. On your commute, listen to personal-development audios by some of the trainers featured in this book. Use the time in your car to recite affirmations or meditate on how your life is going to be once your business becomes a success.

An untrained mind is an expensive hobby. You will have to make some tough decisions to take yourself out of the status quo. This includes the cessation of toxic habits such as consumption of soda, fast food, excess alcohol, processed foods and stimulants. A healthy body is helmed by a healthy mind. Serious entrepreneurs take care of their health so they can be sharp, focused, energized and driven.

I used to be a person who had to watch the news every day and was often lulled into a false sense of anxiety that the world was constantly coming to an end. When I decided to really win in MLM I gave up the television and the newspapers. I dedicated one hour each day to personal development and I still do. I download audios to my iPod and listen to them at the gym or on a run. The world has many people who operate from a place of toxicity and negativity, so there are also many opportunities to participate in mind-numbing toxic behavior.

On the road to becoming a network-marketing millionaire I made the decision to take myself out of the ordinary so I could one day operate in the realm of the extraordinary. You too can take control of your mind and the first step is to get yourself away from the external negativity. You may continue to have naysayers in your life, some of whom share your DNA; however, the more work we do on our minds, the effect others have on us is greatly diminished.

Take control of your mind by resisting the urge to watch the news, read the newspaper or listen to talk radio. Take a 90-day challenge and observe how amazing you feel.

YOUR BURNING DESIRE

I want you to think back to a time when you had something or someone you deeply desired. Your mind was pre-occupied with thoughts of this person or thing. No matter where you were or what you did, the image of this wonderful desire engulfed you like a burning flame on dry wood. Maybe the initial meeting of your current partner evokes such a memory or perhaps it is as material as your big screen TV or a pair of shoes. We all have at least one thing we dream of and hope to never leave this earth without the attainment of it.

My friend Jones, a social worker in Malawi, once shared with me, over a meal, that he only remembers being hungry for the first twenty years of his life. He would wake up with hunger pains in his belly and go to sleep with them. Food became his burning desire as did a life where his children would never know such hunger. Jones put himself through university so he could get a good job and provide. Today, although he does not know hunger, the memory of it haunts him and that propels him forward daily to help those who cannot imagine a full belly.

A burning desire is essential to the pursuit of success in MLM. If your desire is strong enough it will supersede skills; it will get you up in the morning and keep you up at night. Your *raison d'être*, as the French say, or "reason for being," has got to be your bright light or else you will be tempted to quit or settle.

In the business where I achieved seven figures annually and continued to grow my income, I began with a burning desire so strong that I knew only MLM would provide what I needed. After Chris and I downsized our lives, we were living on a household income of about $30,000 per year. We cringed when Avery received birthday party invitations because we could not afford the gift. We were barely staying afloat with our mortgage and car payments and the

MLM that I had been in had been shut down due to health claims. It was a very depressing time in our lives.

That autumn as Avery entered first grade I questioned how much longer we could go on living paycheck to paycheck. I had started using the product line of a two year old MLM company and was getting fantastic results. The compensation plan seemed lucrative, but I was lacking belief in myself, my abilities and my life in general. If it wasn't for a singular event, I am not sure I would have thrown myself into MLM as furiously as I did.

One day Avery's teacher asked the children to bring in something they could read for the following day. That evening, Avery scoured our house and found an Oprah magazine that someone had given to me. She chose a poem by Maya Angelou and read it aloud as I held back tears of pride.

The next day in class, children read a variety of things ranging from their name to a chocolate bar label; no child read more than one sentence. When Avery took her turn and read Maya Angelou without pause, using correct intonation and cadence, I caught the eyes of the teacher and was sure I glimpsed a look of awe.

Afterward, I asked the teacher if Avery could be tested. By the age of six she was already reading chapter books as well as speaking some French, Hebrew and a little Chinese. She fell asleep in class from boredom and I was sure my daughter needed more. The teacher agreed and set up a meeting with the principal. In that meeting the principal seethed in a condescending tone that students like Avery tended to equalize over the year and he would not test her. My interpretation: he wanted to dumb my child down.

That night I went home and decided to build my network-marketing business. I would do whatever it took. I already had certain skills such as presenting, three-way calling, closing and a host of other things. However, I would take them to the next level and I would not even pause until we could afford to send Avery to the best school in our city which cost over $10,000 per year. Yes, I had built network-marketing businesses and seen some results, but this time I would be successful because our little girl's future depended on it.

I ordered the marketing materials for the private school. I put them up where I made my calls. I spent a few minutes each morning visualizing taking her to that school. My husband thought I was crazy, I thought I was sane because I could see no other way to get our baby into a good school.

Ten months later I achieved $10,000 per month on two hours per night. That September we sent Avery to private school and she excelled there. Today we have four children and are committed to the best education and the life experiences they deserve. Thanks to MLM, our children travel, go to great schools and have both of their parents at home. Winning in MLM was never about me, it was about my burning desire to give my child a better life.

Great authors, trainers and leaders can give you the skills, but they cannot give you the desire. Only you know what is going on in your life and you are the only one who can do something about it. Over a decade ago, in reference to MLM, my mentor asked me, "Susan, if not this, then what?" My mind thought of many other possibilities including getting a new job, going back to school and a myriad other things. At that time in my life I was still concocting a Plan B. It took me a few years to embrace the industry and get to a place of really understanding that nothing else would give me the life I desired; only network marketing would pay me over a million dollars per year to be at home with my family.

Let me ask you about your own burning desire. What is that thing that you must have and are willing to make calls for even at 3:00 p.m. on a Friday afternoon instead of checking out? What is that thing that you must achieve that will absolutely transform your life and the lives of those nearest to you? What is that dream that burns inside you and is strong enough to get you through the wall-kicking moments?

Before you do another thing I want you to take a moment and write out something that would absolutely transform your life right now and be a game-changer for the coming year. It could be as simple as having your mortgage paid for by network marketing. Perhaps your child deserves to go to private school or you dream of homeschooling. Maybe retiring yourself or your partner would transform your life. I cannot give you the why but I can contribute to your how.

INSPIRED TO WIN IN MLM ACTION ITEM

What is your burning desire right now? What would be a game changer in your life in the next year?

You have got to have a burning desire that will supersede a lack or perceived lack of skills and push you past apathy.

DECIDE HOW YOU WANT TO SHOW UP IN YOUR LIFE

Now that you have your burning desire, make a decision as to how you want to show up. The most successful people in any room, on any webinar or any conference call also tend to be the most inspired. Decide that you will be the most inspired every day. When you are inspired, you are inspiring. When you are inspiring, others will naturally gravitate toward you.

To be inspired, it is imperative that you surround yourself with inspirational people. Perhaps many of the people in your life are extremely negative. If this is the case you will have to pursue positive role models. Most network-marketing companies offer some kind of support in the form of corporate or leader-driven training. Make sure you plug in.

The wealthiest people in the world tend to be the greatest readers. If you have ever been to or seen photos of luxury homes you will see that almost all of them have a library. Why is this? To be a leader, to be successful, to be inspired (and thus inspire others) means that you will have to build a fortress of inspiration to protect you from the daily assault of negativity.

Make a commitment to read books on personal mastery and financial literacy every day for at least fifteen minutes. We can all carve out time for what we deem important. If your life— like mine— is very full, then purchase audio books and listen to them on your iPod or MP3 player. My friend, Pamela, is an attorney and along with her husband, built a network-marketing business to multiple six figures in 15 months. She also has a five-year-old son. Pamela listens to motivational audios during her commute, at the gym and also over the computer while she is working away on a case or returning emails.

Simply by making the commitment to be inspired every day allows us to find inspiration everywhere, even in movies. One of my favorite movies is *The Pur-*

suit of Happyness, with Will Smith. In this movie, Will plays Chris Gardiner, a dreamer who finds himself living in a shelter with his young son. Chris has a dream of becoming a stock broker and this real life story illustrates how Chris' desire and drive help him to surpass what seem like insurmountable odds. I highly recommend this movie and tend to use pieces at many of my trainings on prospecting.

There are many wonderful movies such as *The Secret, What the Bleep* and others. As a side note, two of the teachers from *The Secret,* Dr. John Gray and Jack Canfield, endorsed my book, *The Have It All Woman.* It is a must-read for women who want to step into a new level of power, are looking for hope and want to unlock the keys to personal success. Many masterful personal-empowerment teachers also have television shows and write for trade publications. I suggest you embrace the industry of personal development so you can show up in a greater, more powerful way.

Inspired to Win in MLM Tip
Decide how you want to show up in your life. When you pour inspiration in, you will pour inspiration out. The more inspiring you are, the more people will naturally gravitate to you.

PROGRAMMING YOUR MIND FOR HIGHER INCOME

When it comes to the attainment of money people tend to struggle because their mind is not programmed for prosperity, but for struggle. In network marketing, many people join for the pursuit of the promise of financial freedom. They attend opportunity meetings where the hope of six and seven-figure incomes are dangled in front of them like a carrot to a hungry rabbit. The reality is that many people are not programmed for six or seven figures. Their financial programming is influenced by the most money they have ever personally made, the incomes of their family and their socio-economic sphere.

It is said that our income is within 80 percent of the five people, outside of our household, with whom we spend the most time. When I first heard this I realized something had to change. I looked at my own social circle and noted that yes, indeed, our incomes were fairly similar. I made a decision to one day have the private phone numbers of seven millionaires in my cell phone and that they would always take and return my call. I knew that by virtue of setting this intention, and pursuing it, my own income would soar.

Some of the trainers in this book are personal, close friends. They are millionaires and multi-millionaires. I encourage you to plug into their trainings and discover how their minds are hardwired for prosperity and not for lack. In order to break free of the bonds of circumstance we must create a new reality. Set an intention today that you too will have at least seven millionaires in your address book and observe how that intention unfolds and who you become in the process.

TRAINING TIP
WITH MASTER TRAINER DAVID WOOD

MINDSET

Only those willing to go too far can possibly discover how far they are willing to go, which makes me wonder, "What if?" What if after reading this article you decide to go further, to take your next step and discover what's lying beyond your current horizon or comfort zone?

Why is it one person seems so unafraid and at home in certain situations of which you're maybe afraid?

Well, next time you're around little tots, watch and listen to their parents, teachers, guardians and you will see the seeds of doubt, fear and uncertainty being lovingly imbedded in their little brains. You will hear phrases like "Be careful, you're going to get hurt" and "Don't roll on the grass, you're going to get dirty" or "Take your hands out of your mouth or you're going to get sick."

Of course, it's not just parents, but the statistics show that the average 15-year-old has heard the word "no" 150,000 times and the word "yes" only 5,000 times, which means that most of us have grown up believing we "can't."

There is a wonderful character in your brain called the "Psycho-Cybernetic Mechanism" which I lovingly call the "Psycho." Its job is to warn you of danger based on your current comfort zone, upbringing, thought patterns and beliefs.

Here is how it works: every time you push against your "current" comfort zone and try new things, your "Psycho" releases chemicals into your brain that are interpreted as fear, uncertainty, doubt or apprehension. Just the slightest seed of doubt can bring you to a full stop or send you into retreat.

Here is the lesson: in order for you to grow, you are going to have to try new things. In order to try new things, you will have to push against your current comfort zone and when you do your "Psycho" will do its job.

So, the next time you're feeling any FEAR, APPREHENSION, DOUBT or UNCERTAINTY you need to get excited and take a step towards your dreams because you are growing.

Get comfortable being uncomfortable and watch your world expand.

Connect with David at www.davidtraining.com

CHAPTER THREE

EIGHT SIMPLE STRATEGIES FOR REPROGRAMMING YOUR MIND

"Always bear in mind that your own resolution to succeed is more important than any other."

-Abraham Lincoln

We only ever decide to do the business of network marketing because we have a desire to succeed. Success in anything is going to require change. At the "Have It All Women's Weekend" and the Power Prospecting Programs that I teach, we define change as simply a new sensation. It is not to be feared, and in order to truly embrace it we must adopt some new habits and ways of being. To paraphrase the Albert Einstein quote at the beginning of this book, we will never truly explore our human potential unless we try something new.

These eight strategies assisted me in becoming a millionaire. We have already touched on some, however in this section we will go into greater detail and set you up to take action now. I would encourage you to do all of these eight things. You may read through once and get started or you may choose to set aside some time each night to work through them. Either way, all eight are equally important, interrelated and absolutely work in reprogramming your mind.

Inspired to Win in MLM Tip
Change is simply a new sensation. If you want more in your life, embrace change. We never truly explore our human potential unless we try something new.

STRATEGY NUMBER ONE
Commit to Daily Personal Development

We all start out on this journey of life as a lump of human potential. Brand new babies are not yet programmed to understand hatred, the fear of success or the fear of rejection. The environment shapes a tiny human and over time we acquire our language and behaviors in relation to our surrounding.

At school, I spent some time in post-graduate studies exploring the psychology of learning. Some theorists suggest we acquire our behavior, views and beliefs from experience, while others suggest that perhaps we bring a coterie of innate operating mechanisms with us on the journey of life. Regardless, the bottom line is this: we all require personal development because likely we have been told "no" or "you can't do this" much more often than we have been told how special, amazing, incredible and powerful we are. Personal development assists in undoing all of the misrepresentations we have about ourselves.

It is said that we experience in the realm of 60,000 thoughts per day. 80 percent of these tend to be negative for the average person. These negative thoughts can sometimes border on the obsessive as we often tend to think the same self-defeating thoughts we have experienced before. Personal development, at the very least, assists us in re-training our mind and taking control of our thoughts. This is imperative if we want to win in MLM.

You will be bombarded with perceived negativity daily so you must "arm" yourself by committing to daily personal development. In the morning, your rested mind is more open to receiving as it has hopefully not been over-stimulated while you sleep. If you have a job, purchase some audio CDs and listen to them in your car instead of the radio or talking on the phone. Audio books are fantastic. It may take you a month or more to read a book however many audio books are condensed to just a few hours. At that rate you can "read" a few books every single month.

Commit to waking up an hour early and starting your day with exercise while listening to something educational and motivational on your iPod. Instead of starting the day with the newspaper, spend at least fifteen minutes reading. Personal development is non-negotiable if you want to win in MLM.

Over the years I have had people criticize my commitment to personal development. I feel sorry for such people for myriad reasons, the first being that if they are not exploring their own potential then they must be complacent people who tend to live without joy. Secondly, the amount of knowledge we garner from books and audios will eventually be turned into financial rewards if we are willing to put it into practice. People who do not believe in personal development are usually both physically and spiritually broke. Never feel that you have to defend your chosen path to a more enlightened you.

My friend Jeff Combs, the master trainer, once became so frustrated with network marketing that he took all of his Jim Rohn audio cassettes out to the dumpster behind his apartment. Not long afterward, he developed a huge sense of loss, and raced out to get the box which thankfully was still there. That was a huge turning point for Jeff; he realized how much more frustrating life might look if it wasn't for personal development. From there, Jeff went from struggling to prosperous and today is one of the most-sought MLM speakers in the world.

INSPIRED TO WIN IN MLM ACTION ITEM

List 3 books/audios that you are committed to reading/listening to in the next 30 days.

*Refer to the reference list at the back of this book.

1.
2.
3.

STRATEGY NUMBER TWO
Use Mt. Everest to Set Your Goals

I want you to imagine a number that is 100 times your current annual income. For example, if you make $50,000 per year, that number would be $5 million. Now I want you to imagine generating this new amount annually. When you think about it, how do you feel? Does it feel possible? Does it feel ridiculous? Does it feel intangible?

I was on the phone with one of the teachers featured in this book. We were talking about being millionaires and he said, "Susan we are capable of making a billion dollars every month." It took me a moment to fathom that much money. The thought of one thousand "million dollars" coming into my bank account every month caused my mind to immediately go to the "how," which is the first indicator that we haven't fully embraced the possibility that we can achieve that level of financial success.

In teaching network marketing to people, I use Mt. Everest to assist them with setting financial markers. This technique has been liberating for many people and here is how it works. I want you to imagine that the level of income that occurs at even 10 times your annual current income is something you can conceive and dream about, but is not a level you have yet experienced. You know that it does exist for people, though it seems like it is a long way from where you are at right now. This goal would be like the summit of Mt. Everest; we know that it exists, yet from the bottom of the mountain that summit is above the clouds.

What we can see from the bottom is Base Camp One and for this is what we should strive. Base Camp One gets us closer to the summit, but we still cannot see it. We feel more confident because we are climbing higher, the view is better and from here we can see Base Camp Two. From Base Camp Two we can now see Base Camp Three. Here we are closer to that cloud layer, the air is crisper, the view to the bottom of the mountain is extraordinary. However, here we are coming too far to turn back.

As we climb from Base Camp to Base Camp, we gain strength, we develop skills, and we appreciate the views and travel far away from the debris at the bottom of the mountain. As we climb higher, the summit comes into view and we confidently head toward it. When we get there, perhaps a little fatigued and out of breath, we pause to look down and realize that although the climb was tough, the view is amazing.

Setting your financial goals in this way will be more tangible than simply heading out for the summit of the mountain. In MLM, many people start out with "summit goals" and only set themselves out to fail because they cannot fathom that level of income. Remember, as you climb farther than the most money you have ever made in your life, the more uncomfortable you may feel. When climbing Mt. Everest, the air gets thinner and thinner and we must adapt.

In the examples on the next page you will see that as we head toward the summit, the multipliers shift so you can additionally shift your ability to fathom this new level of money. Over 90 percent of lottery winners tend to lose all of their money within two years for this very reason. They do not take time to acclimate to their newfound wealth.

In this exercise we are going to set some Base Camp Goals to help you with some meaningful targets. Once you have these, write them out and put them up where you make your calls. This will give you something to focus on and motivate you.

BASE CAMP ONE
Take your current annual income and divide it by 100. This will be the first target to hit in one month in MLM. For example, if you make $50,000 per year, your first monthly target is $500. Round up to the nearest hundred dollars in your personal case.

BASE CAMP TWO
This is double the amount of Base Camp One. In our example it would be $1,000 per month. Once again, round up to the nearest hundred if you have an odd amount.

BASE CAMP THREE
We double the amount again and now we are at $2,000 per month. Round up to the nearest hundred.

BASE CAMP FOUR
We now double that amount and we have basically replaced our monthly income by achieving $4,000 per month. You may consider leaving your job at this point only once you have sustained and grown this income for at least six months.

BASE CAMP FIVE
Once we replace our income, we now must expand our mind to a financial realm greater than what we are accustomed. Take your Base Camp Four amount, divide by two and add it to the Base Camp Four Total. In our example, our Base Camp Four total is $4,000. We divide by two and get $2,000. $2,000 plus $4,000 is $6,000. You now have your Base Camp Five total. Here we may round up to the nearest thousand.

BASE CAMP SIX
Follow the same formula as you did in Base Camp Five. Take your Base Camp Five amount, divide by two and add it to your Base Camp Five total. In our example this would be $6,000 divided by two which is $3,000 and added to $6,000 gives you $9,000 per month. Round up, if necessary, to the nearest thousand.

BASE CAMP SEVEN

Again we follow the same formula. In our example, we would take $9,000 and divide by two, giving us $4,500. Adding it to $9,000 would give us $13,500 per month, rounded up to $14,000. As a note, many network marketers get "stuck" at $10,000 to $20,000 per month. Why? They are simply not programmed to think beyond that.

BASE CAMP EIGHT

Now things are getting exciting. Follow the same formula and round up again if necessary. Thus $14,000 divided by two is $7,000. Add $7,000 to $14,000 and you have $21,000.

BASE CAMP NINE

Once again, follow our formula and take half of your Base Camp Eight amount, add it to your original Base Camp Eight amount and round up. $21,000 divided in half is $10,500, added to our Base Camp Eight amount of $21,000 is $31,500 per month (rounded up to $32,000 per month) or $384,000 per year.

BASE CAMP TEN

Lastly, we once more follow our formula and take the Base Camp Nine amount and divide by two, this time giving us $16,000. We add it to our rounded up Base Camp Nine amount of $32,000 and the total is $48,000 per month which you will find is just slightly more than 10 times your original salary amount of $50,000 per year. In our summit amount we have $576,000 per year.

What happens when you reach the summit? Take a breath and reward your journey. Make sure you have a good tax-planning and financial team in place. You may choose to start the journey all over again, which is what I did. It is a lot of fun. The first million is the hardest. After that you become more adept at creating revenue. The bottom line – start climbing!

STRATEGY NUMBER THREE
The Vision Board

In the movie, *The Secret,* John Assaraf shares his story of his vision board. As he was climbing the entrepreneurial ladder of success, he created vision boards. These boards went into storage and it wasn't until years later, unpacking in his new luxury home in California that he realized he was living in the exact house he had placed on the board. The power of images should not be lost on us. When we see the same images over and over again, our mind begins to reprogram and creates new neural connections that insist these images become the reality of our lives.

I admire the actress Angelina Jolie for her humanitarian work. I have travelled to Cambodia and Ethiopia in my own philanthropic efforts, even working with the same organization that Ms. Jolie is a spokesperson for – the United Nations High Commission on Refugees, or UNHCR. On one of my many vision boards I have a picture of Angelina Jolie on a UNHCR mission. Whenever I look at that board, the image of this woman who also happens to be an Academy Award-winning actress, mother and ambassador for human rights, strikes me.

A few years ago I was asked by the UNHCR to write a paragraph about why I support this incredible organization for a new brochure. When the proof of the marketing document came, my piece was featured alongside a quote by Angelina Jolie and the irony was that very few people were quoted in this piece. It is funny how the universe—who I call God— operates in our lives.

The next year I was in a remote part of Cambodia, on a World Vision mission, and I randomly chose a restaurant to have lunch. After ordering, the server asked me to come with him, there was something he wanted to show me. At the back of the main room was a signed photo of Angelina Jolie from her days filming *Tomb Raider*. This restaurant is where she ate the majority of her meals.

At some point, I would welcome the opportunity to sit down with Ms. Jolie to discuss the plight of women and children in high-risk areas. My work tends to be centered on girls who are at risk of being sold to brothels or in the virgin auctions and it will be wonderful to compare notes.

When you create a vision board, you never know how your life will unfold to reveal the images you have chosen to represent the things you desire in your life. Your vision board is an essential part of your MLM success because it represents a roadmap to freedom. What is at the forefront of our minds is at the forefront of our actions and when these images are in front of you, you act on them. Recall my story, from the previous chapter, about how it was imperative that we send Avery to a special, private school. I had the photos and brochures from the school up on my vision board which I placed on my desk where I made my calls. Whenever I felt frustrated, I looked at that vision board and found inspiration and courage.

My friends, Pam and Kevin, keep their vision board in their bathroom. When I asked them why, Kevin replied, "It is the last place we go at night and the first place we go in the morning." They are massively successful in network marketing and they credit their vision board to keeping them focused. I encourage you to make your own vision board today. If you have an existing team, invite them over to your home and have a vision board party. It will definitely inspire everyone to win in MLM.

STEPS TO CREATING YOUR VISION BOARD

1. You will require a large piece of heavy card paper or a file folder, a glue stick, scissors and magazine or Internet images of everything you desire.

2. Set aside at least one to two hours – as you get going you will not want to stop.

3. You can place the images randomly or you may wish to group them in categories such as health, financial, family, giving back, etc.

4. Place your vision board where you make your calls.

STRATEGY NUMBER FOUR
Affirmations

If you mention the word "affirmations" to a group of people you will inevitably create a divide between those who feel that affirmations work and those who do not. In his book, *The Law of Attraction,* Michael Losier writes that affirmations do not work because the brain views them as a lie. Matthew Ferry, featured in this book, also says that affirmations in a general form are perceived as unbelievable to our conscious mind. On the other side of the argument are people who use daily affirmations as a means to center themselves and firmly believe that there is power in reciting empowering statements over and over again. T. Harv Eker, author of the book Secrets of the Millionaire Mind, believes in the power of affirmations.

Personally, I have used affirmations to keep me on course. In coaching people, and using them myself, I find that affirmations must elicit positive feelings when spoken or they absolutely will not work. Matthew 7:7, in the Bible, reads "Ask and it shall be given." There are many references to the notion that all we need do is ask or visualize and whatever we desire will indeed come to us. Affirmations can be a wonderful form of asking.

One way to look at affirmations is to think of them as a magnet. The more we recite them, the more powerful the magnet. The magnet is pulling our heart's desires closer to us. If we stop reciting our affirmations or lose feeling in them then the magnet weakens and we send a message that we do not really want or intend that thing.

Writing affirmations from a place of "being in process" is additionally helpful. For example, instead of saying, "I make a million dollars per year in network marketing," you would say, "I am in the process of generating a million dollars per year in network marketing." You could also pose a question such as, "Why is it that I am easily in the process of attracting a million dollars per year in network marketing?" I am sure you would agree that the last statement tends to feel better at your core because it is more believable to say that you are in the process and are asking a question as opposed to stating something that isn't true.

Recently, I heard of a gentleman, Kyle, who has created a six-figure income in network marketing. He credits his daily recital of affirmations as being the key game changer in his life. He didn't used to believe in affirmations, but after 30 days he was astounded at how his affirmations began to shift his thinking and thus, his results.

So do affirmations work? The answer is that you will never know until you try for yourself. Take a 30-day challenge to recite your own personal affirmations in the morning, when you wake up, and in the evening, before you go to bed. I have listed some great affirmations below and you can add your own.

Inspired to Win in MLM Tip
Take the 30-Day Challenge and recite your affirmations morning and evening.

AFFIRMATIONS

- I am in the process of becoming a successful network marketer.
- Why is it that I am so easily attracting a seven-figure income in network marketing?
- I am in the process of becoming the leader that people will naturally gravitate towards.
- Every person has a gift to offer me and I graciously accept it.
- I am in the process of creating the family I desire.
- Why is it that I so easily attract incredible, self-motivated, focused, committed, driven and positive leaders to my organization?
- Why is it that my network-marketing income grows effortlessly every month?
- I am in the process of becoming healthy and energized.
- I easily take time every day for gratitude.
- Why is it that money flows effortlessly and easily to me from multiple streams of income?
- I am in the process of becoming a great receiver.
- I easily take action every day toward building the life of my dreams.
- I am in the process of becoming a great listener.
- I ascend to my next level of Base Camp with ease.

INSPIRED TO WIN IN MLM ACTION ITEM

Take a moment and write out at least five Personal Affirmations that you will recite daily over the next 30 days.

1.
2.
3.
4.
5.

STRATEGY NUMBER FIVE
Daily Gratitude

I read a study, not long ago, which found that cancer patients who had a positive outlook and were grateful for their treatment had double the chances of survival. A healthy mindset is directly linked to gratitude and appreciation. When we are able to be grateful for small things, we soon find ourselves attracting even greater things.

Years ago, when I first saw Jim Rohn speak live, he mentioned the power of daily gratitude. Many of the world's leading trainers, including Tony Robbins, teach the power of writing out a minimum of ten things we are grateful for on a daily basis. I have seen people who have been struggling in MLM for months or even years adopt the habit of daily gratitude and suddenly, as if overnight, they begin to enroll new people, have business builders join their team, attract unexpected income, and more.

Daily gratitude is one of the most simple practices to adopt. By "simple," I do not mean easy. Many people overlook gratitude, not realizing that this is one of the most powerful things we can possibly do. In Matthew 13:12 in the American Standard Bible it reads, "For whoever has, to him more shall be given, and he will have an abundance; but whoever does not have, even what he has shall be taken away from him." An interpretation of this could be that to those who perceive all that they have been given, more shall be given and to those who overlook their gifts, all will be taken away.

You may be thinking, "Susan, you are crazy. I am up to my eyeballs in debt, I am in the midst of a health crisis and feeling overwhelmed. What do I have to be grateful for?" I can absolutely relate. When I was diagnosed with MS and my life fell apart it was tough to find things for which I was thankful. What I did was focus on small things such as the sun shining on my face, the sound of my daughter's laughter, the cleansing feeling of a deep breath or the deep blue of the sky. The more I began to appreciate the small things, the more opportunities came my way. I truly believe in the power of gratitude and do not let my head hit the pillow without writing at least ten things to be grateful for.

One year I was speaking at an event with *Chicken Soup for the Soul* co-author Mark Victor Hansen. Mark was sharing his thoughts on goal setting and encouraging the audience to write out thousands of goals. I took this to heart and began a goal book. Instead of merely asking for what I wanted, I decided to write one item of gratitude for every goal. The last time I ran into Mark, I had the book with me. I had 1,600 goals and 1,600 items of gratitude. Mark thought that was pretty impressive.

If you want to shift your mindset, be grateful now. Do not wait for magnificent things to happen in order to appreciate your life; make a decision to be thankful for even the smallest things. The moment you begin this practice of daily gratitude, the moment your mind will shift and you will spend your day in pursuit of more things to appreciate. The most successful people in the world take time for gratitude so let's begin right now and list ten things for which you are grateful.

INSPIRED TO WIN IN MLM ACTION ITEM

Write out ten things that you are grateful for right now.

1.
2.
3.
4.
5.
6.
7.
8.
9.
10.

STRATEGY NUMBER SIX
30-Day Mental and Physical Detox

My friend Jerry Clark is an exceptional motivational speaker. He has worked with audiences all over the world and mentored many successful network marketers. Jerry has worked with great speakers such as Les Brown and the late Jim Rohn. He is a terrific guy with a great sense of humor. Jerry teaches people that if they want to be truly successful in MLM they have got to do a 30-Day Mental Detox. Having done this myself, I can speak to its efficacy.

Your brain and its 100 billion cells process in the neighborhood of 500,000 bits of information every minute. From the air you breathe, to the light around you, to the ambient noise, to the flicker of your eyelashes and the dilation of your pupils, you are an information processing machine more sophisticated than the most powerful computer.

Some of the information your brain processes is essential for survival. For example, your brain will regulate your body to tell you if you are hungry or thirsty or pull your hand away from the hot stove. Other information we process is in response to stimuli that the brain perceives as either negative or positive. For example, we could watch CNN and see the ticker flash saying, "War breaks out in Sierra Leone," and have little effect if we have no relation to that country. If, however, we have travelled to West Africa and witnessed the deep sadness taking place due to corruption in that part of the world, then we may find ourselves feeling overwhelmed with emotions such as anger, frustration and despair.

The thing with media is that stories of war, corruption, murder, rape and deception sell. As human beings we innately gravitate toward such things and these things affect our thoughts. Once our thoughts are affected, our actions will in turn be affected. The news piece that begins your day may inadvertently have a profound impact on your entire day. If you read the news and there is much talk of economic uncertainty, another CEO has been found to be corrupt, and people are losing their jobs at a record pace, you may begin to feel hopeless. This hopelessness may transcend into your prospecting and you may decide to simply not try to connect with people because you have been influenced by what you perceive as negative news.

Henry David Thoreau once said that, "Our perception is our reality." The truth is that your perception is shaped by your experiences and your beliefs. Once you understand that it takes tremendous mental fortitude to stay positive after hearing about death and destruction— an effort that is monumental for even the most well-trained brains— you begin to realize that to win in MLM you will have to limit or totally cut yourself off from such negative stimuli.

I once heard a story about a running-shoe salesman who travels to Africa. Upon his arrival he sees people who appear to be starving, pollution, and hears news of abduction, war and famine. He immediately calls his head office in America and says, "I am coming home. There is no business here. People can barely afford shoes."

Another salesman, from a rival company, travels to the same place. He looks around and sees the same people, hears the same news and immediately calls his head office and says, "It is a gold mine here. Hardly anyone has decent running shoes." Guess who became more prosperous?

We can look at a down economy and think that no one will want to get started with us or we can look at the same economy and think that everyone will be open to looking for a Plan B. Either way, until you have trained your mind to be positive and perceive every challenge as an opportunity then it is imperative that you detox yourself by going for 30 days without reading the newspaper, watching television or listening to talk radio. Observe how your thinking changes—it is quite magnificent.

Lastly, a toxic body leads to a toxic mind. In order to win in MLM you will have to stay sharp so you can seize opportunities. I encourage you to do a good body cleanse at least twice per year. You will have more energy, vitality, mental focus and feel fantastic. I have been cleansing for years. Additionally, take a good multi-vitamin, antioxidants, an omega supplement and drink plenty of water to fuel your body and your brain. Take time for daily exercise and deep-cleansing breath. You can make all of the money in the world but if you do not have your health, what do you have? Take the 30-Day Mental Detox Challenge and be prepared to get to the next level. If the action items sound tough, ask yourself how badly you really want to win in MLM.

INSPIRED TO WIN IN MLM ACTION ITEM
The 30-Day Mental and Physical Detox

- Turn off the television for 30 days.
- Do not read the newspaper.
- Do not listen to talk radio.
- Take a minimum of 30 minutes every day to exercise.
- Drink at least 10 glasses of purified water every day.
- Take time to breathe deeply.
- Listen to empowering audios and read books on personal empowerment.
- Take an excellent multi-vitamin, anti-oxidants and omega supplements.
- Do a deep body cleanse at least twice per year.
- Give up fast food.
- Do not eat processed foods.
- Limit alcohol to once per week.
- Commit to daily gratitude as per Strategy Number Five.

STRATEGY NUMBER SEVEN
The Magic of the Five Choices

Let me ask you this: who are you angry at? Are you disappointed in anyone at this moment? Have you been feeling frustrated in your MLM business? Perhaps you have recently been passed up for a promotion or lost your job and you are bitter that you have landed in MLM at all. Is your spouse or partner unsupportive of your venture? Did your best friend turn down your offer to get started with you? There are so many opportunities to be upset or angry with people and these hurts set us up for more hurts if we continue to carry that proverbial chip on our shoulders.

For years, I was angry at the world. I was even embarrassed that I was in network marketing at all. I had once dreamed of winning the Ironman and being a professional athlete with endorsement deals. On my way to that dream I was diagnosed with MS and eventually became unable to race at all. MS even affected my ability to do my job and eventually MLM went from a "little side business" to a primary business.

It took a long time to see network marketing as a viable career. As I began to understand the various compensation plans, timing and sponsorship I became resentful. No matter which company I was in, I felt that my placement was bad, that other people were favored over me and that my sponsor wasn't doing enough. I fully admit that I was not taking any responsibility for my business. I had already decided that my success was contingent on others and not on me. I operated as the victim instead of the victor.

The result of my negativity was that I struggled in MLM. My struggle naturally did not get me paid. The less money I made, the more negative I became. If this cycle sounds familiar it is no surprise. Many people in the industry fall into this trap only to end up blaming their sponsor, their company or their downline for their lack of success.

To get out of this quagmire of negativity, I made five choices. At first they were not easy to live into and I caught myself more often than not falling into these old patterns of thinking. Eventually they became second nature and they can for you, too. Once I began living into these choices, my income "magically" increased. The faster you embrace the Five Choices, the faster your income in MLM is going to grow.

The Five Choices

1. Only speak about others as if they were present in the room.

2. Take 100 percent responsibility for your own success.

3. Look inward when things are going wrong. Look outward when things are going right.

4. Stop complaining. Release all criticism of yourself and others.

5. Never lie about or embellish the truth about your business to lure people in. This includes what it takes to succeed, how much money you are making or where you are at in your understanding of the business.

INSPIRED TO WIN IN MLM ACTION ITEM

Write out the Five Choices and place them on your bedside table. Commit to them every morning and every evening. Let the magic happen.

STRATEGY NUMBER EIGHT
Find a Mentor

I have been very blessed to share the stage with both Mark Victor Hansen, featured in this book, and Jack Canfield, co-authors of *Chicken Soup for the Soul*. Jack and Mark are phenomenal guys and very wealthy to boot. Early in their career they were both mentored by the famous architect and futurist Buckminster Fuller. Fuller mentored his students to understand that faith was much more powerful than belief and that God was a verb and not a noun. He was an amazing philosopher; a person who both Jack and Mark credit for shaping their destiny. Jack and Mark have gone on to mentor millions of people just like me with their speaking and writing.

Mark is one of the most generous people I know. One year, we did a speaking engagement in Dallas with Jeff Combs. Afterward, Mark spent an hour mentoring me on my writing career. There may be many authors out there, however, only one, to my knowledge, has ever had both a fiction and a non-fiction work on the New York Times' Bestseller List the same week. Mark is that person.

Jim Rohn, the late business philosopher who shaped the landscape of personal development, spoke often about his mentor and the lessons he was taught. Jim's mentor shared wisdom such as the importance of providing service equal to the amount of money we wished to receive, laboring six days and resting one, and other lessons which assisted Jim in becoming the inspirational teacher he was. Jim was my mentor from the stage; his teachings deeply impacted the person I am today— a person who mentors people on a daily basis through conference calls, audios and writing. Jim also mentored Tony Robbins, who would go on to mentor his son, Jairek, who is featured in this book. The power of mentorship is that it is always paid forward.

There are different forms of mentorship. Initially, mentors may come from devouring the pages of empowering books like Robbins' famous, *Awaken the*

Giant Within. Jim Rohn taught me that the New Testament, in the Bible, had the greatest mentor of them all – Christ. Learning from mentors in the form of literature is often the first step for someone entering MLM because it is easily accessible to everyone.

Another form of mentorship is your pastor, rabbi or worship leader. Over 85 percent of American networkers would classify themselves as Christians and it would make sense as the initial foray into MLM requires more faith in the unseen than those without spiritual grounding can perhaps realize. Later in this book we will hear from PK Smith, an amazing mentor to couples in trouble and leaders looking to win in MLM. He spent 25 years as a pastor mentoring the leaders in his congregations and their families.

You can also find mentorship in your company. Perhaps there are leaders who do mentoring calls or run groups. Find out where you can get the mentoring to take you to the next level. In one company, I had the privilege to be on a weekly mentoring call with the top income earner in that company. I was several levels deep in his organization, yet he took me under his wing. His mentorship was a critical part of my success.

Direct mentorship, or one-on-one mentorship, is powerful, though not always free. You may find a mentor to connect one-on-one with you weekly or monthly or perhaps sit down and do a one-time mentoring session. If you are fortunate enough to do this I would urge you to ask great questions. I have done many mentoring sessions and I can usually tell right away who is going to be successful and who isn't. If a person begins by talking about their problems, complaining and spending a great deal of time on what isn't working, I know that they are not likely to see any rewards until they shift their thinking.

If a person makes a million dollars per year then their time is worth about $500 per hour. If you are blessed to sit down or speak to a millionaire, be respectful of their time. Take them to lunch, offer to pay the bill. Ask great questions and above all else, do not complain.

Hiring a great coach is also another form of mentorship. Coaching can run up to $1,000 an hour or more. Some coaches will offer discounted or free trial sessions. Having had coaches myself, I have a few suggestions. Find a coach who has made it in MLM. Some coaches have never made any money in the industry so do your homework. If possible, go to an event or get on a conference call where you can hear that coach. If you resonate with his or her message then it will likely be a great fit.

There are great coaches featured in this book. I would encourage you to check out their websites and find out more about their programs. Regardless of your budget, find a mentor today. Initially it may be in the form of a book, your worship leader or a group setting. If a successful person offers to mentor you, say "Yes." I would not be the person I am today without great mentors. Some of my own students have now become amazing mentors themselves and I learn from them. Mentorship is essential to winning in MLM so find your mentor today.

Inspired to Win in MLM Training Tip
Find a mentor. Every successful individual was mentored by at least one other successful person.

INSPIRED TO WIN IN MLM ACTION ITEM
Finding a Mentor

Here are some great questions when looking for an MLM mentor:

- Has this person been successful in MLM?
- Do you respect this person?
- Are this person's values in alignment with your own?
- What do you hope to learn from your mentor?
- Are you fully willing to do what your mentor suggests?

A FINAL WORD ON MINDSET

As human beings, it is natural to be in constant pursuit of something more. Our very nature has its foundations in desire. There is absolutely nothing wrong in desiring more for your life, and I encourage you to do so. It is only when we associate our self-worth with the fulfillment of desire that we become stuck.

In your network marketing business you will have many opportunities to lose sight of the things that are most important, including your personal health, your relationships and your connection to God or spirit. Getting to the next level of income so you can buy a nicer car or live in a larger home is fine but do not let that define you. Choose to be an amazing person regardless of your bank account, the brand of your shoes or the watch you have. When you decide that you are inspired and represent hope through your vehicle of MLM, you will be amazed at the ease by which these material things simply flow to you.

For a few years I too was caught up in the material aspect of wealth. I wanted the BMW hardtop convertible, the larger home, the Christian Loubiton shoes and more. At that time I associated these things with my worth as a person. I thought that they would impress others. Today, although I have these things, I realize that they do not define me. I appreciate the material manifestations of my millionaire lifestyle, yet the attainment of these things does not inspire me to wake up in the morning.

Financial freedom is about choice. Our bank account is directly programmed to our prosperity mindset. You have the ability to increase your gravitational pull of money at any time you desire and the most sure-fire way to do this is to make a decision that you are enough exactly as you are; that you do not require anything more to be inspiring or to be a better human being. The cars, the watches, the houses and everything else will come with absolute ease once you program your mind to prosperity.

FIELD SUCCESS
BEN S. – FAMILY FREEDOM

I first learned about the industry of network marketing at the age of 19, while in college. A family member was involved in a company and initially I joined as a way to make some extra money while going to school. It wasn't until after I graduated from college that I found my passion and decided to take it seriously. I went full-time five years later and I never looked back.

Network marketing has given us complete life freedom. Not just financial and time but family freedom as well. My kids are growing up never knowing what it's like to have parents work outside the home. My wife and I are able to volunteer in our second-grader's class twice a week. We're able to be there for our children when most parents are not. That is something that we are really proud of. But the biggest thing that network marketing has given us is the freedom to live. So many people are bogged down by the stresses of everyday life that they aren't able to live their life. Being able to simply enjoy each day is a blessing and this industry has given us the ability to do that. Our mission is to help others have the same experience!

FIELD SUCCESS
DR. RICK L. – NO MORE TRADING TIME FOR DOLLARS

As a health care professional, I was always trading time for money. If I wasn't in the office, then I wasn't earning my professional degree potential.

Holidays were difficult to take because expenses would never take a holiday.

A client of mine introduced me to MLM and I was surprised that a business professional was doing that type of business. So I listened, then let go of my own prejudgment and this created a whole new world of opportunity.

It has allowed me to enter into a business partnership with my friends, family, and other professionals. It also allowed me to give and receive support from people in different parts of the world.

This residual business revenue has allowed me to decrease my clinical hours, sell one of my clinics to my associate and to stop trading time for money.

Now I spend more time with my family, take holidays without fear and I am able to help other people create and reach their goals and dreams.

Sincerely,

Dr. Rick L., D.C.

TRAINING TIP
WITH NY TIMES BEST-SELLING AUTHOR AND MASTER TRAINER T. HARV EKER

All of us have a personal money blueprint ingrained in our subconscious minds that will determine our financial lives. If you want to truly be inspired to win in MLM, you must shift your money blueprint.

Have you ever wondered why some people seem to get rich easily, while others are destined for a life of financial struggle? Is the difference found in their education, intelligence, skills, timing, work habits, contacts, luck, or their choice of jobs, businesses or investments?

The shocking answer is none of the above!

No doubt you've read other books, listened to tapes or CDs, gone to courses and learned about numerous money systems, whether they are in real estate, stocks or business. But what happened? For most people, not much! They get a short blast of energy, and then it's back to the status quo.

Finally, there's an answer. It's simple, it's law, and you're not going to circumvent it. It all comes down to this: If you subconscious "financial blueprint" is not set for success, nothing you learn, nothing you know and nothing you do will make much of a difference. I'll explain more about this later.

MY OBSESSION WITH BECOMING A SUCCESS

Like many of you, I supposedly had a lot of potential but had little to show for it. I read all the books, listened to all the tapes and went to all the seminars. I really, really, really wanted to be successful. I don't know whether it was the money, the freedom, the sense of achievement or just to prove I was good enough in my parents' eyes, but I was almost obsessed with becoming a success.

After leaving college during my first year, I spent the next twelve years trying to make ends meet. Any money I made, I lost. I really couldn't rub two nickels together. I thought that I was fairly intelligent and a good person, and I couldn't understand why the one thing that I wanted, financial success, completely eluded me.

Then, as luck would have it, I got some advice from a rich friend of my father, a wealthy man in many ways. He was a strongly principled person who had a really big heart. He said to me, "Harv, if you want to be successful at business, you need to do what successful business people do. Rich people think the same thoughts and take similar actions, albeit in different vehicles. So by reading, studying and modeling them you can pick up what they do."

It was time to put what I learned to the test. I opened my next business, which was one of the first retail fitness stores in all of North America. And using the principles I learned, I became a millionaire in only two-and-a-half years. The business was so successful that I opened ten stores in that time alone.

After selling the company, I took a few years off to refine my strategies and began doing one-on-one business consulting. And today, my sole mission is to teach these same principles to people throughout North America via my Millionaire Mind Seminar program.

I would like to share with you a little about how each of us is conditioned to think and act about money. I'll help demystify for you why some people are destined to be rich and others are destined for a life of struggle. You'll understand the root causes of success, mediocrity or financial failure and begin changing your financial future for the better.

WHAT IS YOUR MONEY BLUEPRINT?

One of the things I say in my book *Secrets of the Millionaire Mind: Mastering the Inner Game of Wealth,* as well as on radio and television, is give me five minutes with anyone and I can predict their financial future for the rest of their life. How? I identify their money blueprint.

Each of us has a personal money blueprint already ingrained in our subconscious mind that will determine our financial life. What that means is you can know everything about business, marketing, communications, negotiation or real estate, for example, but if your subconscious money blueprint isn't preset to a high level of success, you will never amass a large amount of money.

We've all heard of Donald Trump and what he has accomplished. Here is a multibillionaire who at one point lost everything, and within two years, he's got it all back and more. Why? His money blueprint is set for "high." On the other side of the coin, we have lottery winners. They win millions of dollars and within five years virtually half of them are back where they started. Why? Their money blueprint is set for "low."

HOW YOUR MONEY BLUEPRINT IS FORMED

What we have to realize is that we are all taught and conditioned about how to deal with money. Unfortunately, many of us were taught by people who didn't have a lot of money, so their way of thinking about money became our natural and automatic way to think.

Your mind is nothing more than a storage cabinet. In this mental file cabinet you file and store information. Where does this information come from? It comes from your past programming. Your past programming determines every thought that forms in your mind.

So the questions becomes, "How are we conditioned?" We are conditioned in three primary ways in every arena of life, including money:

- The first influence–Verbal programming: What did you hear when you were young?
- The second influence–Modeling: What did you see when you were young?

- The third influence–Specific incidents: What did you experience about money, success and rich people when you were young?

THE FIRST INFLUENCE: VERBAL PROGRAMMING

Did you ever hear phrases like, "Money is the root of all evil," "Save your money for a rainy day," or that rich people are greedy, criminals or "filthy rich"? You may have been told you have to work hard to make money. In my household, every time I asked my father for any money I'd hear him scream, "What am I made of…money?"

Every statement you heard about money when you were young remains lodged in your subconscious mind as part of the blueprint that is running your financial life. Naturally, you don't even have to think about it. You don't even see it. You go to your money file, pick it out and do what you're supposed to do with it. That's because your subconscious conditioning determines your thinking. Your thinking determines your decisions, and your decisions determine your actions, which eventually determine your outcomes.

THE SECOND INFLUENCE: MODELING

The second way we are conditioned is called modeling. There is a saying, "Monkey see, monkey do." Generally, we will tend to be exactly like one or a combination of both of our parents in the arena of money.

So the question is, what were your parents like around money when you were growing up? Did they manage money well or did they mismanage it? Were they spenders or were they savers? Were they shrewd investors or were they non-investors? Was money always a struggle in your home or was it a source of joy and ease? Whatever your answers, you will be very similar to that. Although most of us would hate to admit it, there's more than a grain of truth in the old saying, "The apple doesn't fall far from the tree."

On the other side of the coin, some of us are exactly the opposite of one or both parents when it comes to money. Many people who come from poor families become angry and rebellious about it. Often they either go out and get rich or at least have the motivation to do so. But there's one little hiccup. Whether such people get rich or work very hard trying to become successful, they usually aren't happy. Why? Money and anger become linked in their minds, and the more money such individuals have or strive for, the angrier they get.

The reason or motivation you have for making money or creating success is vital. If your motivation for acquiring money or success comes from a nonsupportive root such as fear, anger or the need to prove something about yourself, your money will never bring you happiness.

THE THIRD INFLUENCE: SPECIFIC INCIDENTS

The primary way we are conditioned is by specific incidents. What money-related experiences did you have when you were young? These experiences are extremely important because they shape the beliefs, or rather the illusions, you now live by.

Let me give you an example. A woman who was an operating room nurse attended the Millionaire Mind Intensive Seminar. "Josey" had an excellent income, but somehow she always spent all of her money. When we dug a little deeper, she revealed a memory of when she was 11 years old at a Chinese restaurant with her parents and sister. Her mom and dad were having yet another bitter argument about money. Her dad was standing up, screaming and slamming his fist on the table. She remembers him turning red, then blue, and then falling to the floor from a heart attack. She was on the swim team at school and had CPR training, which she administered, but to no avail. Her father died in her arms.

Since that day, Josey's mind linked money with pain. It's no wonder, then, that as an adult, she subconsciously got rid of all of her money in an effort to get rid of her pain. It's also interesting to note that she became a nurse. Why? Is it possible she was still trying to save her dad?

WHAT IS YOUR MONEY BLUEPRINT SET FOR?

Now it's time to answer the million-dollar question: What is your current money and success blueprint, and what results is it subconsciously moving you toward? Are you set for success, mediocrity or financial failure? Are you programmed for struggle or for ease around money? Are you set for working hard for your money or working in balance? Are you set for having a high income, a moderate income or low income? Are you programmed for saving money or for spending money? Are you programmed for managing your money well or mismanaging it?

As I stated earlier, your money blueprint will determine your financial life—and even your personal life. If you're a woman whose money blueprint is set for low, chances are you'll attract a man who is also set for low so you can stay in your financial comfort zone and validate your blueprint. If you're a man who is set for low, chances are you'll attract a woman who is a spender and gets rid of all your money, so you can stay in your financial comfort zone and validate your blueprint.

So again, how can you tell what your money blueprint is set for? One of the most obvious ways is to look at your results. Look at your bank account. Look at your income. Look at your net worth. Look at your success with investments. Look at your business success. Your blueprint is like a thermostat. If the temperature of the room is 72 degrees, chances are good that the thermostat is set for 72 degrees.

THE ROOTS CREATE THE FRUITS

The only way to significantly change the temperature in the room is to reset the thermostat. In the same way, the only way to change your level of financial success permanently is to reset your financial thermostat, otherwise known as your money blueprint.

In life, our fruits are called our results. So what do we tend to do? Most of us focus even more attention on the fruits, our results. But what actually creates those fruits? The seeds and the roots, that's what.

What's under the ground creates what's above it. What's invisible creates what's visible. So what does that mean? It means if you want to change the fruits, you will first have to change the roots. If you want to change the visible, you must first change the invisible.

In every forest, on every farm, in every orchard on Earth, what's under the ground creates what's above the ground. That's why focusing your attention on the fruits you've already grown is futile. You cannot change the fruits already hanging on the tree. You can, however, change tomorrow's fruits. But to do so, you'll have to dig below the ground and strengthen the roots.

TRAINING TIP
BY MASTER TRAINER TODD FALCONE

HOW DO I MAKE IT HAPPEN?

The BIG question everyone asks themselves once they've gotten involved in network marketing is, "How do I make it happen?" Everyone wants the answer, but it seems too few ever find it. The reality is that the answer is right there in front of them...all of them, and it always has been. Look in the mirror. The answer lies within. In order to guarantee your success in this profession, you first must start by making a decision to do it.

Once you decide, it's done. The decision has been made. I challenge anyone reading this to dig inside and ask yourself if you've really made the DECISION to do it. Just because someone has an ID number in a company doesn't mean they've actually made the real decision to do it. Once you CHOOSE to do it and then back it up with ACTION, it's only a matter of time before your life dramatically changes.

Success begins when you decide to be successful. Becoming massively successful in network marketing is really quite simple. Find a company that fits your heart, make a decision to do it (that means there are no outs), start taking action (prospect and expose), get better (work on you), and never stop taking action.

Let me put it to you this way: Let's say you have an opportunity in front of you, one that when pursued would absolutely change the quality and the direction of your life forever. Your life would never be the same. You'd have everything you've ever wanted. All you have to do is act. In other words, make the decision to DO it, and all you've ever wanted would be yours with no chances for failure. If you actually DID it, you'd be assured success. Would you then do it? That's where you are right now.

Todd Falcone is a 20+ year network marketing expert and trainer. For more information, visit www.ToddFalcone.com and receive a 30% discount on any of his physical audio training products by using the coupon code: power.

CHAPTER FOUR

CREATING A PLAN THAT WORKS AND WORK THE PLAN

"We are what we repeatedly do. Excellence, then, is not an act, but a habit."

-Aristotle

IS YOUR BUSINESS A BUSINESS OR A HOBBY?

Now that you are developing your winning mindset, creating some great habits and living your potential as a person inspired to win in MLM, it is time to get down to business. Ultimately we get paid on our habits. If you have ten-dollar habits, expect a ten-dollar income. If you want to make a million dollars a year or more, then you need to have million-dollar habits.

In MLM it is often said that if you treat your business like a business you will be paid as a business owner. If you treat your business like a hobby you will make a hobby income. They call it NetWORK marketing for a reason—because it is not Net-Play marketing. A winning mindset will magnetize great people to you, and your habits will take your team to the summit. Basically, when it comes to winning in MLM I like the following equation:

MINDSET + HABITS = RESULTS

PART-TIME OR FULL-TIME

As mentioned in Chapter One, the vast majority of people participate in our industry on a part-time basis. A part-time commitment is really ten hours per week; anything less than that means you are not really serious. I have helped many people achieve six figures part-time; however, they are disciplined, focused, have the right mindset and have six figure habits. They do not watch television or aimlessly surf the Internet, and they do not complain. They take care of their health and they SHOW UP.

I actually see people do more with ten committed hours than forty undisciplined ones. In my last company, it took me ten months to get to $10,000 per month on ten hours per week. I had a full-time job, two kids and a husband who worked over seventy hours per week. In other words, I did not have a lot of time.

If you are in MLM full-time and it is considered your profession, then you are likely spending twenty or more dedicated hours each week to your business. My friend Jeff Combs says that the majority of people who call themselves "full-time" are really only "part-time." In other words, they are fooling themselves into thinking that they are actually committing to income-producing activities for 5–8 hours/day when the reality is that they are emailing, researching and talking on the phone to current distributors and not really doing anything to generate more sales volume.

Decide right now if you are full-time or part-time. Either way, you can never be an all-the-timer or you will most likely burn out. If you have a day job, a family and other obligations, then expect to be part-time and surrender until you reach Base Camp 5. If you are full-time and not getting the results you are seeking, then you most likely need to shift your mindset and change your habits. No matter where you are, you require a schedule that works, so let's get started and create a winning schedule for the professional networker you are.

CREATING A SCHEDULE THAT WORKS FOR YOU

In many of my books, including the *Have It All Woman* and *MLM Woman*, I stress the importance of a schedule. Man or woman, part-time or full-time, you need a schedule that is going to align with both your goals and your life. Not long ago I received a call from a woman who was already achieving six figures in MLM. She had a one-year-old and a new baby on the way. She was overwhelmed and exhausted.

I asked her to share her schedule with me. "Schedule?" she replied. "What schedule?" She went on to tell me that she was in the throws of building her business and was taking calls day and night, seven days per week. No wonder she was agitated. She would sit down for dinner, and if the phone would ring, she would get up and take the call. She would be trying to put her son down for a nap, and if the phone would ring, she would take the call. Her business was running her and not the other way around.

I then asked her why her business was more important than her husband and son. She insisted that it was not that way. I proceeded to connect her with her actions. When she left the dinner table to take calls, she sent a loud-and-clear message that business was more important than family. When she took her distributors' calls at all hours of the day, her message was that her time was not valuable and that she wasn't important.

After some mentoring, I asked her to create a schedule with some sacred boundaries. I asked her to fill in time for her husband, time to exercise, time connecting with God and time to "fill her well." We can never take water from a well that is empty, and we cannot ever give more from a place that is barren. If we are "all-the-timers" in our business, we will soon become resentful and be resented by those closest to us.

After this lovely gal changed her habits, created a new schedule and set some boundaries, her income soon doubled. I also asked her to establish a separate business phone line so she could discern personal family calls from business ones. Up until this time, even with a six-figure income, this woman did not have a dedicated phone line. Setting your schedule is key if you want to portray a professional image; conveying your schedule in the form of office hours on your incoming voicemail message is also essential.

People often ask me how I write books, travel to third-world countries, run two companies, speak at events and raise four children. The answer is simple—I have a schedule that works for my life. I live the schedule, and the schedule liberates me to do many things.

Generally people waste a tremendous amount of time on things that do not produce income or benefit their overall emotional, physical and spiritual health. Trust me—you will not leave this Earth wishing you had watched more *Dancing With the Stars* re-runs. A study found that when people worked on a project and kept their email open simultaneously, they wasted fifteen minutes every time they attempted to go from email back to the project. Even dedicating specific times each day to return emails can liberate your time.

I don't care what anyone says, I believe in multitasking. When I am at the hair salon, the gym, doing errands or at the yoga studio, I am prospecting and connecting. If you are building a business part-time, you will have to become efficient and develop your networking skills by utilizing day-to-day activities to generate leads. Anyone who tells me that they cannot talk to people about their business doesn't truly believe in their business, plain and simple. If you are passionate about something and believe in it, you will talk about it, end of the story.

Whether you are full-time or part-time, you have to make the most of your time. If you want to earn six figures part-time, then figure out how much money your time is worth and treat it with respect. If you intend to generate $10,000/month on 10 hours/week then your time is worth $250/hour. Can you afford to waste that time on convincing people to get started or stay in your business? Can you afford to watch television during peak production hours? The answer is no. Treat your time like it is worth $250–$500/hour, and it soon will be.

In creating your own schedule you will want to include the following:

- Time to prospect for new business builders.

- Time to train your new people.

- Time for personal development.

- Time for exercise. (I listen to personal development while I am working out.)

- Time for general errands such as groceries, banking, etc.

- A date night with your partner or potential partner.

- Time to re-fuel. We take Sundays completely off.

- Time for administration, including emails, responding to voicemails, etc.

Lastly, once you set your schedule, let everyone know exactly what it is. Leave a professional voicemail that outlines your office hours. This will create boundaries and send a loud and clear message to the world that you mean business. If you go outside of your schedule, then do so by choice and not by guilt or obligation. Your schedule will liberate you, and best of all, you can always modify it if it isn't working.

INSPIRED TO WIN IN MLM ACTION ITEM
Create Your Schedule

List out all of your current obligations, including a job, shuttling
children, any committees you have, going to the grocery store, etc.
Now, ask yourself if there is anything you can give up or if possible,
hire someone else to do. As soon as I hit a six-figure income, I hired
a housekeeper. At $300,000/year I hired an assistant, and I have
never looked back. Chances are there are things in your life you can
delegate. Get your schedule done today.

BE THE PERSON THAT YOU WOULD ENROLL WITH

So, let me ask you the million-dollar question—would you enroll with you? If I
spent 24 hours with you, what would I see? Are you punctual? Are you professional? Do you procrastinate? Do you follow-up? What is your attitude like?

In MLM it is very common to hear, "look for leaders." I like to say, "Be the
leader you would sign-up with first if you want to attract great leaders." I do not
believe in faking anything; however, you can step into a new level of leadership
by creating some better habits. Whether you make seven figures or have never
made a penny in the industry, I want you to ask yourself if you would indeed
enroll with you right now in the way that you are operating. I believe that this
is an important question and one that we should all use from time to time to
simply check in.

A great litmus test is to list the top five qualities of people you are seeking to
partner with in your enterprise and then measure those characteristics against
yourself. You can score your own traits on a scale of 1–10, with "1" being absolutely not possessing that quality to "10" being that you absolutely do possess
this quality. Let's get started.

Five Characteristics That I Am Seeking in Business Partners versus My Rating

Fill out the characteristics that you are seeking:

Characteristic	My Score on a Scale of 1–10
1.	1 2 3 4 5 6 7 8 9 10
2.	1 2 3 4 5 6 7 8 9 10
3.	1 2 3 4 5 6 7 8 9 10
4.	1 2 3 4 5 6 7 8 9 10
5.	1 2 3 4 5 6 7 8 9 10

So how did you do? Can you see the areas of improvement you can choose to make? We know that like attracts like. The more you seek to improve your character, develop exceptional habits and live an authentic life, the faster the right people are going to show up and start in your enterprise.

SOCIAL MEDIA AND YOU

In this age of Facebook and Twitter, which I am sure will be obsolete in a matter of years, we are experiencing wonderful opportunities to connect with old classmates, prospect for new business partners and even train our people. Your social media presence is also your brand. Being aware of your perception is key if you want to win in MLM.

Not long ago there was a dispute by a teacher who was terminated for posting "lascivious" photos of herself on Facebook. The school principal saw this girl having a glass of wine on holiday in Italy and a mug of beer in Germany and thought that this was not appropriate for the school. Whether wrong or right, it is all a matter of perception. Everyone from employers to your grade-school bully may follow your social media presence.

As you grow in MLM, your profile will grow. People will begin to "Google" you and your social media history may come up. I tell my children to only post things they would want the world to know forever and be extremely cautious. Recently, my daughter unlocked her Facebook access. A person I do not even know messaged me through Facebook to suggest that her personal photos were inappropriate. Even though my daughter was taking some pictures with her friends, those were linked to me. You see, even your children and your spouse are linked to your social media presence.

If you are going to use social media as a tool, then I strongly suggest the following:

- Never post anything negative such as, "I am upset at my daughter," or "So-and-so burned me." Whatever you post is the image you convey. If you are having a rough day, do not let everyone know.

- Do not make every single post about your company. That gets old fast.

- Do not post extremely personal photos and be cautious of photos that are taken of you. People photograph me at various events, and yes, they all end up on Facebook.

- Do use social media as a tool to generate leads. Post interest generating remarks such as, "Just got off the most inspirational call," or "So excited to be feeling better now than I did 20 years ago."

- Represent yourself professionally, and do not use your company logo instead of a photo. Have a good photograph taken.

- Schedule social media into a specific part of the day. You can waste a great deal of time simply reading other people's posts, watching videos or playing games.

SO YOU WANT RESULTS

Lastly, if you truly want results, you have got to clean up your habits. Million-dollar habits will eventually yield a million-dollar income. Interview successful people and ask them about their habits. Ask them how they plan their day, schedule their time and manage themselves within that time. When I decided to win in MLM, I made a commitment to have seven figure habits and that includes learning to say the words "yes" and "no."

People will always ask you to do things, and if you are to say "yes," make sure you are doing so without guilt or a false sense of obligation. To win in MLM also means sometimes saying "no," even if you feel that people may be disappointed. Once you begin to live into your schedule and decide what is and is not going to serve you, you can commit your time to taking action to get to the next level of base camp.

At the end of the day, we are ultimately paid for recruiting and helping our people recruit. We are paid for retention and increasing sales volume. Almost every business in the world is run on a similar platform: find customers, keep customers and assist customers with purchasing more.

Your habits have got to match your desires. Daily, steady, consistent, productive habits will win over massive action every time. Be the person you would enroll with. Commit to doing whatever it takes within your boundaries, and lastly, make a decision to treat your time as if it were worth $500/hour or more because someday it will be.

FIELD SUCCESS
PAM AND KEVIN B.
SIX FIGURES PART-TIME

We are proof that anyone can succeed in the network marketing industry. When we were first introduced to network marketing, we were unfamiliar with the concept. Okay, the truth is we did not know what network marketing was. Kevin was working fifty-plus hours per week as a police officer, and I was working fifty to sixty hours a week as a lawyer. This was in addition to the time we spent on our real estate business. Little time was left over for family time—our most valuable time. Network marketing has allowed us to make a healthy shift. Within six months I replaced my six-figure salary and have since "retired" as a lawyer, allowing me to spend time with my husband and son. Kevin is months, instead of years, away from retiring as a police officer. Imagine how many years that will add to our lives! We treat our network marketing business as a business—not a job. Our networking business pays us an incredible residual income, not an hourly wage.

TRAINING TIP
WITH MASTER TRAINER MATTHEW FERRY

HOW TO CREATE A PLAN FOR YOUR NEW LIFE IN THE MLM BUSINESS

Your mind is not your friend. It will convince you that you don't need to write down your goals. Even worse, the life you already have will trap you if you don't do something to break free of your current orbit.

Here's the good news! Your life alters to fit your written commitments. I've coached more then 8,000 people and found that a person who is mentally clear and focused on a goal, can accomplish as much as 80 percent of what he/she writes down.

The first step is a vision letter. In your imagination, stand one year in the future and look back over the year. Describe in detail your life as if it had already happened perfectly. Create detailed descriptions in the following categories: physical health, mental/emotional state, spirituality, family life, primary relationship, business, personal finances, social life, recreational activities, and the contributions you made. Describe it as if it has already happened.

The second step is to break down the actionable steps. Some of the results you described had actions that must be taken in the first quarter in order to produce the results you described in the letter. Don't worry about planning each quarter in advance. Just start with the first quarter.

Answer these questions:

1. What needs to get done?

2. What do you need to start working on?

3. What do you need to learn about?

4. Who do you need to meet?

Step three is to create a structure so that you look at this list of goals every couple weeks and create mini-action plans to get them done. It's fun! Your life becomes your creation versus a reaction. Try it today. For a sample vision letter and fourteen more inspiring strategies for free go to www.15strategies.com

Bio: Matthew Ferry is a revealer, illuminator and awakener. He uses multimedia and coaching to present a point of view that creates instant transformation in people's lives. He has penned three transformational books including *Creating Sales Velocity, Instant Inspiration* and *The Truth Virus.* For more ideas on how to shift your life now, visit www.matthewferry.com

CHAPTER FIVE

THE PEOPLE BUSINESS

"If you can dream it, then you can achieve it. You will get all you want in life if you help enough other people get what they want."

-Zig Ziglar

PEOPLE WHO NEED PEOPLE

It has been said time and again that network marketing is "the people business." Regardless of which method you choose to build with, including the cold market, warm market, leads, ads or online, you will require real, living, breathing human beings to build your business. I have met many people who want to hide behind their computer and never talk to people. Even worse, I have met people who advertise businesses that claim to never require people to interact with others. The other trainers in this book would agree when I say that ultimately you are going to have to build relationships with people if you hope to create a sustainable, successful MLM legacy.

Human nature innately requires human connection for our own survival. We are wired to need to be with others. MLM, at its best, utilizes our fundamental need for relationships and creates lasting bonds where all parties benefit. The beauty of network marketing is that some of our best friends and greatest relationships may actually come from people who enter our business.

We need one another to survive, and we need others to thrive in MLM. You may find a great recruiting platform using only the Internet; however, at some point you will have to pick up the phone and connect with people to build relationships. One of my great friends, Marlene, found me online and enrolled in my business. We didn't meet face-to-face for almost a year; however, during that time we built our relationship over the phone. We have been business partners for years. I have stayed at her home, we have done yoga, and we have gone to church together. If I had simply allowed Marlene to sign up and never built the relationship, she likely would not still be in business with me today.

We are in the people business. To win in MLM you have got to be prepared to build relationships with people.

The bottom line is that if you want to win in MLM, you must be inspired to connect with people. Human beings are truly fascinating creatures. Take time to discover the dreams and goals of another. Find out about people's strengths and their vision. All it takes is a handful of great people who are committed to becoming your lifelong business partners to truly make a significant income in any network marketing compensation plan.

GETTING THE BEST OUT OF PEOPLE

One of my mentors taught me that to get the best out of people you have to be willing to pour greatness into them. Instead of focusing on what other people are doing wrong, focus instead on what they are doing right. When we focus on what others do well, they will do more of the same. If we strive only to correct or criticize another, we will never pull the best from them.

The same mentor, who taught me about people, constantly poured belief into me. On every phone call he would tell me that one day everyone in our company would know my name. He pointed out only what I did well, even if it was something fairly small. I found myself consistently wanting to do more of the things that he felt I was good at. Not once, in almost a decade, has he ever criticized me. He is one of those charismatic people who bring out the best in others.

To build a successful network marketing business, you want to be that leader who inspires others to consistently give their personal best. In my most recent build, I only recruited eighty people to make my first million dollars. My husband often observes that I tend to believe in people to a fault, often believing in them more than they believe in themselves. The mark of a great leader is to have enough belief that their people can borrow from it until they develop belief in themselves.

To get the best out of people you have got to pour your best into people.

TO WIN IN MLM YOU HAVE TO UNDERSTAND THE NUMBERS

The first time I saw the Geometric Progression of Numbers I realized that I had found a very forgiving industry. If I committed to recruiting five people who then recruited five and so on, I could make a tremendous amount of money. In a perfect world, none of these people would ever drop out; however, the world isn't perfect and attrition will occur. As the chart below illustrates, we can actually succeed only 10 percent of the time and still make a significant income.

GEOMETRIC GROWTH - MULTIPLE OF 5	
LEVELS	NUMBER OF PEOPLE
1	5
2	25
3	125
4	625
5	3,125
6	15,625
7	78,125

Let's use another example to illustrate how simple it is to make a six or seven figure income in MLM. To understand this example you must know that the average payout in network marketing is approximately 5 percent. Some companies will payout a higher percentage on the "front line" or personally enrolled;

however, the percentage tends to decrease with depth. Other companies, binary compensation plans for example, may pay a higher percentage of volume on the minor leg or pay only when the legs are equal. There are approximately four main types of compensation plans in MLM with slight variations and permutations therein.

A BRIEF OVERVIEW OF COMPENSATION PLAN TYPES

Stair Step - You sponsor wide on your front line and are paid on depth based on the volume in each "leg." Some of the oldest compensation plans are in the Stair Step Breakaway format, whereby if one of your leaders begins to generate more volume than you do, they "breakaway," and you are no longer paid on their volume.

Unilevel - You sponsor wide and are paid on limited depth. There are no breakaways; however, you are cut off anywhere between 5–9 levels deep.

Matrix - If you remember the Rubik's Cube, you can comprehend the Matrix plan. Essentially you have a limited amount of width and depth. As you sponsor, you fill in your matrix, and the volume associated with each of those spots fuels your paycheck.

Binary - The Binary plan often has two legs, pays unlimited depth but has a cap on how much money you can make with the two legs.

I have worked in all of the above plans. I made the most money in a binary, though I have had friends who have made significant income in all of the various structures. Regardless of the structure, if we return to our example we will see that the type of compensation plan is not as significant as the total number of people in the organization.

Let's imagine that you recruit ten people who all order $100 in products. Now let's say that you encourage each of them to recruit ten people who order $100, and these people duplicate and do the same. Those people now duplicate, and we suddenly have a significant team as per the example below.

Level	Total People	Sales Volume $
Level One	10	1,000
Level Two	100	10,000
Level Three	1,000	100,000
Level Four	10,000	1,000,000

So you duplicated four times and had an organization that generated one million dollars in sales volume. Now, let's imagine that you received 5 percent of that, which is $50,000. However with monthly reorder programs, this didn't happen just once; it continued to happen month after month. That is the beauty of MLM. Everyone, in this example, only recruited ten people. Even if 90 percent of your organization dropped out, this would still be $5,000/month in residual income. The above example could occur in any one of the four key types of compensation plans.

Ultimately, make it your focus to understand the geometric progression of numbers. When you recruit people, make sure you help them also recruit people. The more you do this, the more money you will make. There is no residual income if you are the only one recruiting.

Inspired to Win in MLM Tip
Understand the geometric progression of numbers.

BECOME A PROFESSIONAL TALENT SCOUT

Here is the bad news—people will drop out of your organization. There are a variety of reasons for this occurrence, though often people quit because their habits and mindset are not in alignment with the goals they have set for themselves. Because people will leave, you must commit to constantly be connecting with new people about your service or product.

If you committed to talking to three people every day about your business, you would have connected with 1,000 at the end of one year. If 90 percent said "no," you would still recruit 100. That may be all it takes to create a significant income.

To achieve a seven-figure annual income in MLM, I committed to daily prospecting. When I recruited three or four people, I would work with them, train them, help them enroll their initial people and then go recruiting again. The top leaders in our industry are constantly "talent scouting" as I call it.

The statistic in sales is that the majority of closes occur after the fourth follow-up and yet the majority of salespeople give up before the fourth call. When you find someone who has the characteristics you are seeking, become a professional talent scout and commit to following up until they tell you not to.

Inspired to Win in MLM Tip
Be a professional talent scout and commit to connecting with a minimum of three people every day about your opportunity.

CREATE A SYSTEM FOR RECRUITING AND CLOSING

I have heard that by profession teachers and engineers make the most money in network marketing. One possible reason is that teachers and engineers are very systematic, that is, they are trained to do the same thing over and over again. If you want to win in MLM, you have got to have systems for recruiting and closing. Fundamentally a system is only as good as the people who follow it, and people only tend to follow a system that produces results.

Whether you are using home presentations, three-way calls, leads, ads or building online, you have got to be systematic in your approach, and you have to be duplicatable. If you are doing elaborate product presentations, designing your own websites and materials without your team being able to do the same things, you will not likely make very much money. The best systems I have ever seen tend to be the simplest in that they are easy to follow and anyone can replicate them regardless of skill level.

Take a moment right now and answer the following questions with regard to your systems. If you do not have the answer, I highly recommend you connect with a successful person in your company to help you create a system that works in your business.

QUESTIONS ABOUT YOUR SYSTEMS FOR PROSPECTING AND CLOSING

1. Do you have a system to use to connect with people in your day-to-day life?
2. Do you have a system to connect with leads?
3. Do you use an auto-responder?
4. Do you have a system to invite people to events?
5. Do you have people who can help you close a sale?
6. Do you have a system to follow-up?
7. Are you using a contact manager?
8. Do you have marketing materials and websites that you feel comfortable using for your prospects?
9. Do you have live webinars or closing calls that you can bring people to?
10. Do you have resources to answer specific questions about your product or service?

INSPIRED TO WIN IN MLM ACTION ITEM

Write out your system for prospecting.

_____

_____

_____

Write out your system for closing.

_____

_____

_____

Inspired to Win in MLM Tip
You have got to have systems. You will only duplicate if your systems are easy to follow and do not require any special skills.

SPONSORSHIP MEANS TAKING RESPONSIBILITY

Your business is not about recruiting as many people as you can and, like throwing spaghetti against the wall, hoping some stick. When you sponsor someone, take responsibility. Train and mentor them. Every time you enroll a new person commit to matching energy with them for at least ninety days. Often the top recruiter in any company is not the top income earner. Yes, you want to continuously be sponsoring; however, if you are not training your people to do what you do, you will never duplicate.

A TOUR OF THE BUFFET

I am grateful that my dad, an engineer, taught me to continually look for multiple streams of income. I officially joined my first company at age 24, although I had spent a few years as a pre-teen accompanying my stepmom to network marketing in-home presentations. By the time I joined that initial company, I was well versed in sales; however, my understanding of the industry was extremely limited.

The person who enrolled me with that first $1,400 package simply told me to find other people to do the same and retail the products from the order. What he did not do was plug me in to any training, teach me about the compensation plan or tell me what it takes to really win. I have nothing but compassion for this person. Perhaps he didn't know what he was doing or maybe he was just excited to make the sale. Either way, I learned a valuable lesson from the experience and that was to make sure that every person I ever enroll is plugged in to everything the company has to offer. It is not up to me to decide for them how much they need to know to be successful, since as adults we can make decisions on what is right for us.

I love to share the example that a network marketing business is much like a buffet. If you have ever visited an all-you-can eat buffet then this will make total sense. Watch anyone approach a buffet and you will see that the first thing they usually do is walk the length of it to see what is offered. Once they find the particular selection, they often beeline for that area. When they start eating, they decide how hungry they are, what they want to eat and how many visits they will make. The same is true in our industry.

In any solid company there are numerous resources; there are often archived calls, webinars, podcasts, videos, documents and much more. There are usually event listings and training components. Our responsibility is to assist our new person with taking a tour of what our company has to offer and then allowing the individual to decide what they want to partake in.

As individuals, the same is true of us; we must take 100-percent responsibility to find out what a company has to offer in terms of training and support. I have witnessed many rogue "leaders" who discourage their people from plugging in to a company's resources. The end result is that team members never create loyalty to the company and only to the individual. Although this may be effective for a certain period of time, the lasting effect is that team members miss out on all of the incentives, promotions and trainings a company has to offer. The bottom line is this: in order to win in MLM you have got to be plugged in to the company. Your team will only plug in to the extent that you do.

It is extremely seductive to allow our perceptions to limit the experience of another. We may wrongly assume that our new product user is just that, a person who only wants the products. We never know what is truly going on in the life of another. Do not pre-judge someone; allow them to come to their own conclusions. Be respectful but always present everything your company has to offer, including the business side of things. You never know when your next product user could become your best business builder.

At the time of my $1,400 product purchase, I was going through a very difficult time in my life. I had been diagnosed with a degenerative disease, my marriage was falling apart, and I would soon lose my business. Within months I found myself with over $100,000 in debt, jobless, homeless and a single mom. Could network marketing have reconciled that situation? I will never know. I do believe that if I had been given a full perspective of what I had, perhaps I would have been empowered to make different decisions. I live a life of no regrets; however, based on my experience, with new enrollees, I choose to present the entire picture and know that it is not up to me to decide how much a person wants to know about the business side of things.

The person who did finally "take me on a tour of the buffet" also introduced me to the company where I would go on to enjoy seven figures annually. She showed me everything network marketing had to offer, including personal growth, financial freedom and the ability to truly discover who I was as a person. My mentor not only ensured that I was on company calls, exploring the company resources and attending corporate events, she also set me up on a schedule of personal development books including some of my favorites*: *The Power of Focus, Rich Dad Poor Dad, Think and Grow Rich* and many others.

I am so grateful that my mentor took the time to show me what the industry had to offer. Network marketing has strengthened my character; I have been able to overcome both physical and financial obstacles. Both my husband and I have spent a tremendous amount of time in personal development first as students and now as trainers. This industry has allowed us to truly become free and that would never have happened if we hadn't been exposed to everything MLM has to offer.

Network marketing isn't just about great products or fantastic opportunities; it is also about the challenge to grow personally and empower others. The thing I would love to share is that if you commit to this industry, the industry will commit to you. You can become a person who is positive, inspiring and a true leader. You can empower others to become more. Make a decision to plug yourself in to your company and your industry, and choose to take responsibility for everyone you enroll to ensure that they too realize all of the invaluable resources that are available.

*See the recommended reading section at the back of this book.

Inspired to Win in MLM Tip
Do not pre-judge a person's desire to know more about the business, and do not assume that your product users are solely interested in the products.

FIELD SUCCESS
TERRY P. – FROM SINGLE MOM TO MULTIPLE SIX FIGURES

I was introduced to network marketing four years ago, and I am so grateful to my friend that introduced me to it because my life has been enriched in so many ways.

Before I started network marketing, my life was no picnic. I struggled with many things. I was tired, stressed out, divorced, broke and a single mom of three young children. I worried about money all the time. How was I going to make ends meet? Would I have to sell my house? Move to a different town? What was going to happen? How was I going to survive?

Well that feels like a different world now, thank goodness! I am so in love with this industry; it has given me more than words can describe. I am free. I am happy. I am at peace. I can mold my future to be what I want it to be. I can live the life I choose. It's so great in so many ways!

The best part of all is that I get to take others along with me. This is such a win/win industry. For those who are willing to put in some effort on the front end of their MLM business, there is much to gain. These gains are realized along the way. It's hard to completely understand all of it unless you have done it. Once the money is there and you don't have debts or worries about money, it's time to reflect and look at what else you have gained. How many people have you helped to follow in your footsteps? How many lives have you helped change for the better? These are just some of the questions that run through me as I look back on what has happened in the past four years. This happens automatically if you have a good system to follow. You model the system and train it! Set the example, set the pace and your people will follow.

The people that I have met in this industry are incredible. They have so much integrity. They are open. I have met some of my best friends since joining MLM in the last four years. It's so great too because you are working together so you spend time together. You are on the same page and automatically have so much in common. There is also a lot of personal growth training that is offered, and I have to say that it is invaluable and allows you to grow much faster than you would without it.

The training and the automatic learning that comes with being in this industry have helped me to be more open and honest with people. I don't concern myself with what others think of me—I know it's really not about me. I have learned to accept all kinds of different people and look for the good in everyone. It is there—everyone has good in them. I have learned the power of motivation, belief and consistent action. I understand that when I do things that make me uncomfortable, I am doing something really great—I am growing and becoming a better person!

TRAINING TIP
WITH RELATIONSHIP AND LEADERSHIP SPECIALIST P.K. SMITH

Co-Creation

Multiplying Your Strengths Against the Strengths of Your People for Maximum Results

A number of years ago I spent an entire day listening to Susan Sly, as well as another great leader in the MLM industry, tell an eager audience how they had successfully built an enormous team in a reasonably short period of time. I was enthralled by their heart-warming illustrations and the inspiring examples of families and individuals whose futures improved immeasurably because of their collaboration with these two leaders. Their example of humility, insight and selfless investment in others struck a cord in my heart and mind. As I was traveling back from the event a light bulb switched on in my head that encapsulated what their stories of personal success were depicting. I called it Co-Creation.

The evolution of the Co-Creation principles has been less intentional than you might imagine. As I was training MLM novices and veterans alike, the feedback I received was always the same. The Co-Creation principles were resonating with so many people in a positive way. Eventually I was asked to travel to a brand new team and just teach the Co-Creation principles as a stand-alone training.

All the members of the team were new to the MLM industry. They were enjoying the products of their new company, and they were seeing the contagious nature of the MLM opportunity. But they could also look far enough into the future to realize that they needed to learn an effective working model soon, before frustration and attrition infected their team.

So I spent a day with this amazing group of leaders. The average leadership number in the room was much higher than the typical MLM gathering. Most of the participants had honed their leadership skills in high pressure and enormously responsible careers. Frankly, it was a privilege just to have the honor of spending the day with this exceptional group of influencers.

I spent the day sharing the Co-Creation principles with that team along with the necessary leadership principles they would require. In my twenty-five years of mentoring leaders I have learned that no matter what the industry may be or the purpose of the organization, the number one factor which determines a group's legacy is their ignoring or investing in developing principle-driven leadership. Most people live their lives based on emotions and feelings. Leaders learn, either innately or intentionally, to live their lives by predetermined principles. This is what separates the sheep from the goats. It is the difference between experiencing frustrated failure and embracing long-term success.

In the months that followed, that team enjoyed tremendous success within their industry.

Now let me be clear, embracing Co-Creation is not a lottery ticket for success. There is no magic scratch pad on your training manual. The principles simply guide your efforts so that instead of developing your business by sheer effort and exertion, by adding to your influence and growth daily, you will transform into someone who multiplies your effectiveness and your results within an empowered team.

I believe that Co-Creation is the next evolved social and financial architecture. That is why when someone asks me if my business is related to the MLM industry I don't apologize. I energize. My face lights up like a Christmas tree and I respond, "Absolutely, why would I want to waste my time with anything less?"

You see there are three ways to bring influence and wealth into your life. Most people only are aware of two.

You can earn it.

You get a job and someone you don't know, and probably don't like, hands you a check. After taxes, insurance and union dues, you make do with whatever is left. Our education system points our young people toward this lifestyle. It also happens to be the segment of the economy with the fewest deductions so that this is the heaviest taxed portion of the population. What a surprise.

You can Make it.

A small slice of the population dares to leave the earners, and they strike out to start their own business. Small businesses are the backbone of the Western economy, but they are also very challenging. You trade a service or product with another business or the general public and then after payroll, insurance, taxes, capital investment and market wavering, you have whatever is left to call your personal income.

The intimidation factor of moving from being an earner to the mental and emotional strain of being a maker is what holds so many people back from even dipping their toe in the MLM industry. What most people don't know is that a well-designed MLM should avoid most, if not all, of these headaches. That is because a well-designed MLM should invite the entrepreneur into the world of Co-Creation.

When you Co-Create, you multiply your gifts and ingenuity with the other members of your empowered team to create a finished product of success that is so much more than the sum of its parts. The key is to be deliberately finding the greatness in each member of your team and allowing for your special greatness to enhance and exponentially increase the results that each person can receive into their lives.

When you choose to Co-Create, you move to a new economic reality that exists beyond market downsizing, beyond restrictions due to geographic distances or even cultural challenges.

When you choose to Co-Create, you learn to return to the days of your childhood, where dreams are encouraged and are enjoyed by the entire team.

When you choose to Co-Create, you leave the herd and you strike out on your own with a team of like-minded leaders who experience no limits to their potential impact.

When you choose to Co-Create, you become unemployable. It is too much to handle to a step back in time and space and live your life under such a limiting system.

It has been my privilege to Co-Create with Susan Sly for a number of years now. Our Co-Creating energy has influenced thousands of people in business around the world as well as thousands of people in humanitarian advances in the Third World. I am excited to see that so many of my Co-Creation graduates are following our example by also investing in the lives of the needlessly impoverished people of the Third World. I have shared my mission statement so many times that I can see people moving their lips with me as I recite it at every event I train at.

"I choose to Co-Create wealth in the First World, to erase the pain of the Third World. THERE IS ONE WORLD TOO MANY!"

The Co-Creation movement is building like a "Benevolent Tsunami." Each week I get another request to come and teach the Co-Creation principles, and it has become my grand obsession. I invite you to join the new social architecture that will revolutionize how we view our lives, our businesses and our potential legacy as we Co-Create this planet into a better place to live for everyone.

If you want to know how to become a Co-Creating Master, contact us at www.stepintoyourpower.com and mention you were directed to the site from this book. We have a special introductory coaching offer for you. Remember to mention how you heard about the site to receive this special gift from Step Into Your Power.

UNLOCKING THE POWER OF BEING
A CO-CREATING COUPLE

I serve as the chaplain for our local police force. Most of what I do there is marriage counseling. Police officers experience a divorce rate that is 300 percent higher than the average person. It is fulfilling and intense work. My success with challenged couples has spread so that today I help couples connected to other police services all over North America.

But the strain of the police officer's lifestyle is not the only one that tears at the foundation of our marriages. When a couple reinvents themselves with a new business opportunity, there is also a new strain, and often, it is an unfamiliar one that they are ill prepared for. When anything new is introduced, there is an inherent fear that sweeps into a relationship like an ominous fog. Because of this reality there are steps that are required to solidify your marriage to face the future fearlessly.

1. Understand that schedules will have to be adjusted.
The MLM industry does not take place during typical business hours. That will mean making and keeping a schedule that incorporates the new demands without ignoring the needs of a healthy marriage.

Most people do not live by a schedule that is this deliberate, so it feels odd to be planning a date night, a weekend getaway or marriage enrichment class. You need to learn to do this. A MLM business can hit your home like pancake mix and fill in any unprotected space. If you don't want to feel resistance from your spouse then protect their time and space with you so that they feel more cared for rather than less.

2. Personal growth is not optional so keep your spouse abreast of your transformation.
Many people share the Cliffs notes of their personal growth and then can't understand why they feel like they are drifting apart from their spouse. It is because of their unintentional communication with them. Don't stop sharing the changes that are taking place in

your life just because your partner doesn't seem overly enthused with your information. Keep them in the loop to ensure that they know where to find you when something does strike their interest.

Be careful about developing emotional ties within the MLM industry that exclude your spouse. Great news should be shared first with your spouse because they are the love of your life, not because they clap the loudest. You made vows of exclusive priority, so keep them, even with your MLM development.

I have counseled too many broken hearts that when they retell the tale of their marital ship wreck it started with a breakdown in communication. If you disengage from them verbally and that won't be your only problem real soon. The desired goal is a fully engaged spouse that will stand by you.

3. Focus on what your partner is great at.

It is easy to spot how your spouse isn't supporting your new venture. It is relationally lazy to look for what is wrong and what needs to improve. It takes effort to spot and congratulate what is right and what works.

Does your spouse help with the household activities so you have more time to build your business? Tell them how much that means to you.

Does your spouse cover childcare responsibilities while you travel or talk on the phone? Tell them how much that means to you.

Does your spouse play the role of guinea pig while you try a new product or a new connecting technique? Tell them how much that means to you.

Does your spouse tell other people about this new business venture you are embracing? Tell them how much that means to you.

Does your spouse congratulate any level of success you achieve? Tell them how much that means to you.

That was not a pass/fail checklist. It is a reminder of how much your spouse may already be doing to support your MLM venture. You may have been missing their attempts at support. You may have missed the opportunity to say thank you. Put this book down right now and go thank them for what they are doing that is helpful.

Are you back now? Good. Now what can we do about what your partner isn't doing to assist you? If you did what I just asked you, then you have already begun. It does not matter what gender you are, we all respond better to positive drawing than to negative driving. That means the better you get at reinforcing helpful behavior, the more of it you will experience.

You need to understand that taking either a pity posture or control tact will blow up in your face. Your partner is probably more than a little intimidated and fearful of what you are doing. They may or may not understand the MLM industry. They will not understand and appreciate it more if you attempt to force them to do so.

Stop leaving MLM books on the nightstand or wrapping them as Christmas presents. Simply enjoy the support and understanding they share with you today and exuberantly express your appreciation. Then get back to work.

Determine to passionately congratulate support and hold yourself to only answer the questions your partner is asking about the MLM industry. Most times less is more. Let them be asking for more information rather than trying to escape the sound of your voice.

Remember that at the end of the day you made vows for your spouse and intentions for your business. Don't sublet your vows for your goals. Vows matter. They express the greatness of who you are as a person. Don't diminish your greatness by confusing your priorities.

P.K. Smith is available for relationship and leadership coaching. Contact P.K. Smith at kevin@stepintoyourpower.com or visit www.stepintoyourpower.com and ask for the special relationships coaching offer attached with this book. We are committed at Step Into Your Power to offer "Holistic Success" to business families around the world and that means enjoying more than just a healthy bank account, we want healthy homes for you all as well. So please remember to mention you were directed to the site from this book to receive this free offer.

CHAPTER SIX
CREATING YOUR MLM DYNASTY

"It's hard to see your own face without a mirror."

-Dr. Phil McGraw

WHAT DO YOU WANT TO BE KNOWN FOR IN MLM?

At many intensive personal empowerment courses people are asked to write their own eulogy. The same exercise is relevant in MLM. Even though the force is millions of people strong, it is still a relatively small industry. When I decided to become a network marketing millionaire, I wanted to be known not for the money I was making, but for the people I had helped become successful. In Proverbs it says that "wisdom shall be known by her children;" in MLM this couldn't be more applicable.

If someone were to write about you as a network marketer what would they say? Whose life, other than yours, have you impacted? Who have you helped? Who has benefited just from knowing you? What impact have you made by being in MLM? How has your family, your community or the world been blessed by your network marketing career?

If I took a good look in the mirror, I would definitely be able to say that many others have benefited because I have been inspired to win in MLM. From helping Chris retire so we could be at home with the kids to supporting the economy and hiring people to work for us on a full- and part-time basis, to paying massive amounts of taxes to support infrastructure to our work in Cambodia and Africa, we can say that network marketing has been a gift to children rescued from brothels and remote villages in Malawi where we have built schools and supported projects to benefit local communities. To find out more about our philanthropic projects please visit www.stepintoyourpower.com.

On another note, becoming millionaires in network marketing only occurred because we helped other people succeed—and not just the people in our organization. I regularly do training calls and speak at events with people from a wide range of companies. I truly believe that when we serve with a full heart we are rewarded.

I want you to take a good look in the mirror and ask yourself how being in network marketing is affecting others. Is it positive or negative? Are you making an impact? Most importantly, how would you like it to be? Take a few minutes to do the following exercise. You can be at the helm of your own MLM dynasty, and regardless of where you are at today, you can start right now by living as the person I know you can be.

MLM ACTION ITEM

Imagine that it is five years from now and you are being interviewed by a magazine for entrepreneurs. The magazine is writing a story about all of your accomplishments in network marketing. You are asked about your triumphs, how the industry has benefited your family, your community and others. Write the magazine article and do not leave anything out.

CONCLUSION – NO EXCUSES

The pages of this book have been filled with the tools to inspire you to win in MLM. You have received tips on mindset, habits and developing relationships. You have been given industry information that has hopefully built your belief and understanding. All of the knowledge in the world means nothing until you apply it and turn it into wisdom.

The challenge with many people is that they spend more time learning than doing. Their income is a direct reflection of this. I want you to be a great learner but more importantly I want you to be a great doer. People will never judge us by what we say as much as by what we do; our actions really do speak louder than our words.

In your journey to MLM success you will encounter many challenges; there will be times you want to quit. You will be faced with obstacles and want to give up. If you are truly inspired you will never stop; you will have a "no excuses" mentality.

MLM can liberate you and your family; it can provide long-term residual income. That will only happen if you commit to daily action over the course of years and not months. When you choose to move forward no matter what, that is when the magic begins. You suddenly find that people begin to show up in your organization with that "no excuses" mentality and momentum occurs.

I encourage you to embrace MLM as a profession. Make a decision to seek out inspiration daily, focus on developing a winning mindset and do not quit...ever. I know that you are capable of achieving great things in your network marketing business and that you are equipped. Go for your dreams with passion and enthusiasm and be inspired to win in MLM.

FIELD SUCCESS
JANNA S. – FINANCIAL DEVASTATION
TO FINANCIAL FREEDOM

I was determined to create my life financial stability ever since immigration to Canada from former USSR at the age of thirty-two. In pursuit of it, I turned many hobbies of mine to the business. For over twenty-five years I worked very hard, starting from my own two hairstyling salons for five years, then my own handicraft and fashion designs stores for another five. After that I owned a gourmet health food products manufacturing business for another five, and then I worked as a real estate broker and at a wellness center. called "Not Just Another Hotel" in Costa Rica.

What was missing every time was that in those enterprises I had hoped to achieve financial stability, but on the contrary, I was always in huge debt, and I had no chance to have any free time. Developing and supporting those businesses took all of my time. I had to compromise on my sleep and spending time with my only child, so I couldn't even think of having a second child.

At the end of the day my health was hugely compromised. I would have been prescription dependent for the rest of my life if it wasn't for a friend who I hadn't seen or spoken with for over fifteen years. That friend suddenly called me one day and introduced me to the Wellness System, which happened to be distributed through Network Marketing.

Wow! What I discovered made me fall in love with the MLM industry. Here are a number of things:

Educate yourself and learn about leadership. Owning my business was my choice, and this opportunity involved no high cost, or hardly a cost to start up. It offered me the leverage, time flexibility and freedom to live my dreams, from smaller to larger and larger. And now, at the age of sixty-nine, I feel that the best is yet to come!

I have it all now. I worked very hard for a year and a half to create a six-figure reoccurring income. I've grown into a person who I like way more than I did before, and I have helped a number of people transform the quality of their lives, physically and financially, and I gained life-long loving relationships.

I've met many incredibly driven people who were willing to teach the secrets of this industry so others could succeed. I have met people from all walks of life who were willing to work on improving their own physical and financial health.

I had to learn more about my own discipline, which was not easy, since I didn't have a store to go to. I worked out of my home. I had to improve my communication skills; I had to learn how to teach others. In the beginning I just did not know how to find people who were ready to do what it takes to create profound changes in their lives. It took me quite some time to realize that I was spending too much time rescuing people who didn't want to do the work on themselves. In other words, I wanted it more for them than they wanted it for themselves.

TRAINING TIP
BY NY TIMES BEST-SELLING AUTHOR OF CHICKEN SOUP FOR THE SOUL™ AUTHOR MARK VICTOR HANSEN

The Eight-Step Process to Better Asking
by Mark Victor Hansen

Your success in MLM hinges on becoming a master asker. In my studies and writing on success in books such as *The One Minute Millionaire, Chicken Soup for the Soul, Richest Kids in America* and others, I have found that the most successful people on the planet are able to ask for business without attachment to the outcome.

But just how do you go about getting started asking? Here are the primary action steps to take:

1. Act as if you expect to get it. It is of primary importance that your state of thinking contains a solid level of certainty and expectation when you ask. This state of mind will affect everything else—your body posture, eye contact, tone of voice and choice of words. Think for a moment—you've been in situations when you've asked and had every certainty that you would receive exactly what you were asking for. Remember how you felt then? Keep that in your mind with every request you make.

2. Ask someone who can give it to you. Before you ask someone for something, make an assessment of whether or not they will be able to give it to you. Some people are very qualified and motivated to help. Others just aren't capable of delivering—watch people and review that capacity. Have you ever seen them capable of delivering what you're about to ask them, or are you just hoping the potential is there?

3. Get the other person's full attention. Your request deserves that respect! If the person cannot give you his or her full attention, set up an appointment, ask to talk during the commercial break, or ask them to schedule time for you in the very near future.

4. Be clear and specific. Be as concise as you possibly can in your requests. Ask for what you want, not for what you don't want. At the same time, be careful what you ask for—more often than not, you get exactly what you've requested!

5. Ask from the heart. You can have anything you want if you want it desperately enough! Keep that unbridled passion for your purpose, project or goal stirring in your soul as you begin to ask, and maintain eye contact throughout the entire asking process. This further establishes your integrity, trustworthiness and passion on the subject.

6. Ask with humor and creativity. Humor captures our attention and breaks down our defenses. Creativity disarms our resistance and opens our minds to new possibilities.

7. Give something to get something. As Zig Ziglar says, "You can get everything in life you want if you will just help enough other people get what they want." When you're asking, always be sure to explain what's in it for them, how they benefit and win because they've acted positively on your request.

8. Ask repeatedly. If someone says, "No!" you say "Next!" Expect "No's" even on a repeated basis from the same people you're asking. Your tenaciousness and perseverance will undoubtedly pay off.

So You've Asked and They Still Say "No"—Now what?

Don't lose your cool when you're faced with resistance! A powerful request can only be powerful if you're also willing to be declined. Ask with authority, prepare yourself for a "no," be gracious in receiving that "no," then make one of two choices:

- Ask the person with whom you just made the request to help you with a solution. They may know someone who CAN give you a "yes" and, given some freedom and respect from you, they often wander their own way into providing your "yes."

- Walk away without burning your bridges. You probably just came across someone who feasibly could not help you. The world is much too small and inter-connected to lash out at even one person.

Mark Victor Hansen is a master trainer and multiple NY Times bestselling author. He has impacted the lives of millions of people on the planet. Mark has a tremendous heart of service. You deserve to learn from Mark. Visit www.markvictorhansen.com.

TRAINING TIP
WITH MASTER TRAINER JAIREK ROBBINS

Create Time for Yourself to Step into a More Successful and Fulfilling Life

Spending my entire life immersed in the personal development industry has provided an insider's view to see people transform their lives, business, emotions and health. I would say that the number one most important trait a person can develop if they want to accomplish HUGE goals is the ability to identify, breakdown and apply patterns. There are consistent patterns that all of us use to create results in our lives, and consistent patterns we all use to create failure. If you took a moment and wrote down your top ten achievements in life, and the steps you took in order to achieve each of them, you would begin to see a pattern of behavior (action), thoughts and emotions that lead you to what you call "success." Once you have identified your personal strategy/pattern for success you have the opportunity to repeat the pattern and test it to see when and where it actually works (you might be surprised!).

The number one pattern I have seen in people who are unbelievably successful and fulfilled in their life is the pattern of consistently taking time for themselves. Here are a few key steps that you can use each morning to start your day powerfully:

1. Moving and breathing (3–5 min). Get up, take a walk and start breathing! I recommend breathing in through your nose four deep breaths at a time and powerfully breathing out through your mouth those same four breaths.

2. Gratitude (3–5 min). Now, while still walking, take some time to think of EVERYTHING that you are grateful for. Family, friends, the breath in your lungs, the sights, the sounds, etc. All can be sources of gratitude. Just flood your body with gratitude. It helps if you say these things out loud.

3. Visualization (3–5 min). This next step requires you to begin to imagine all the things you would like to have happen in your life in the next few days, weeks, months and years. Personally I like to just speak out loud and state all of the amazing experiences I want to take part in, people I want to meet, etc. Say these statements out loud as if they have already happened.

4. Exercise (15–30+ min). This next segment is when you kick it in gear and take a jog, run, bike ride… something that will get your heart pumping and fill your body with energy!

5. CELEBRATE! (As long as you'd like!) When you get back from your exercise, make sure to take the time and actually celebrate the victory you just created and the progress you have made for your mind and body!

Jairek Robbins is a personal coach, speaker and entrepreneur. Visit www.JairekRobbins.com for more information.

"It is not the magnitude of our actions but the amount of love that is put into them that matters."

-Mother Teresa

GLOSSARY OF TERMS

Affiliate, Distributor, Associate - A person who joins a company. Someone who can earn income from sponsoring other people.

Downline - Refers to to team member who are or can be financially linked to the associate.

Upline - Refers to people who are above and financially linked to the associate.

Cross-line - Refers to people, in a company, who are not financially linked to the associate.

Pre-Launch - The period of time where a company opens to when it officially begins to ship products or deliver on services.

Launch - The period of time when the products/services are actually available to distributors.

FDA - Food and Drug Administration – USA

FTC - Federal Trade Commission – USA

BV - Business Volume – each product or service in a company has an associated dollar to volume ratio. There are various names in individual companies.

RECOMMENDED READING/ AUDIOS AND MEDIA

The Power of Focus by Jack Canfield, Mark Victor Hansen and Les Hewitt
Rich Dad Poor Dad by Robert Kiyosaki
The Richest Man in Babylon by George S. Clason
The Alchemist by Paulo Coelho
Think and Grow Rich by Napoleon Hill
Your First Year in Network Marketing by Mark Yarnell
MLM Woman by Susan Sly and Suzan Hart
Excuses Be Gone by Wayne Dyer
Think Big and Kick Ass by Donald Trump and Bill Zanker
Why We Want You to Be Rich by Donald Trump and Robert Kiyosaki
The Pursuit of Happyness with Will Smith – available on DVD
The Secret by Rhonda Byrne
Secrets of the Millionaire Mind by T. Harv Eker

RECOMMENDED WEBSITES

Susan Sly's Site	www.stepintoyourpower.com
Mark Victor Hansen	www.markvictorhansen.com
Todd Falcone	www.toddfalcone.com
Jeff Combs	www.goldenmastermind.com
Erica Combs	www.goldenmastermind.com
David Wood	www.davidtraining.com
P.K. Smith	www.stepintoyourpower.com
Jairek Robbins	www.jairekrobbins.com
T. Harv Eker	www.peakpotentials.com

ABOUT THE AUTHOR

Susan Sly is a successful entrepreneur, author, speaker, master trainer, certified nutritional consultant, certified trainer and coach with over 17 years of experience in health and wellness. She has also generated more than $60 million in sales in the industry of network marketing and become a seven-figure annual income earner.

Susan has competed for Team Canada six times both in Track and Field and Duathlon. She has competed in two World Championships. She placed in the top 10 in the pro division of the Ironman in Malaysia in 2001. In 2007 Susan completed in the Boston Marathon.

Susan is an in-demand motivational speaker and has shared the stage with Mark Victor Hansen, Jim Rohn and more. Susan is a success coach and speaker who has helped co-create numerous six and multiple six-figure earners.

From the years of 1997 to present, Susan has been featured on television, radio, print media and has speaking engagements booked into next year.

Susan has four children, ranging from 1 to 13 years, and is the devoted wife to her life partner Chris Arkeveld. Susan and Chris dedicate time to giving back and are currently involved in a fundraising project with World Vision to support a trauma center for girls rescued from brothels and sexual trauma in Cambodia. Susan and Chris also sponsor 20 children through World Vision.

Susan is the author of the bestselling book the *Have It All Woman, MLM Woman* and the co-author of the new book *The Ultimate Guide to Power Prospecting*. She is the founder of the Have It All Woman's Weekend where women undergo three days of life-changing personal empowerment. Susan is the President and CEO of Step Into Your Power Productions, a company dedicated to teaching individuals how to create more abundance in their lives.

Her website is www.stepintoyourpower.com.

INSPIRED TO WIN IN MLM